Exploring Christianity

Jesus and the Birth of the Church

Gwyneth Windsor
and John Hughes

HEINEMANN
EDUCATIONAL

Heinemann Educational,
a division of Heinemann Educational Books Ltd,
Halley Court, Jordan Hill, Oxford OX2 8EJ

OXFORD LONDON EDINBURGH
MADRID ATHENS BOLOGNA PARIS
MELBOURNE SYDNEY AUCKLAND SINGAPORE
TOKYO IBADAN NAIROBI HARARE GABORONE
PORTSMOUTH NH (USA)

First published 1990

91 92 93 94 95   12 11 10 9 8 7 6 5 4 3

British Library Cataloguing in Publication Data
Windsor, Gwyneth
  Jesus and the birth of the church.
  1. Jesus Christ
  I. Title II. Hughes, John III. Series
  232

ISBN 0 435 30270 1

Designed and produced by VAP Publishing Services, Kidlington, Oxon

Printed and bound in Spain by Mateu Cromo

Acknowledgements
Thanks are due to Religious Studies Consultant W. Owen Cole,
Roger Owen and Janey Graham for commenting on the manuscript.

The publishers would like to thank the following for permission to
reproduce photographs: J. Allan Cash Ltd. pp. 13, 29(E), 69, 74;
Ancient Art and Architecture Collection/Ronald Sheridan pp. 63 (H),
80 (A and B); Andes Press Agency/Carlos Reyes pp. 11 (top), 55 (H),
68 (C), 76 (B); Associated Press pp. 71 (centre), 72; Barnaby's Picture
Library pp. 5, 55 (I), 71 (bottom); The Bridgeman Art Library pp. 29 (D),
62 (D), 62 (E); Camera Press Ltd. pp. 11 (bottom), 39, 40 (C), 62 (G),
87, 95 (G); J. Catling Allen pp. 58 (D), 84 (B); The Church's Ministry
among the Jews p. 54 (D); C.M. Dixon p. 92 (B); Keith Ellis Collection
p. 55 (F); Greg Evans Photo Library p. 48 (B); Rex Features/Ben Alofs
p. 68 (B); Rex Features p. 89; Paul Ferraby/Torch Trust for the Blind
p. 45 (C); Format Photographers p. 95 (H); Glasgow Art Gallery and
Museum p. 62 (F); Sally and Richard Greenhill pp. 45 (D), 94 (E); Sonia
Halliday Photographs pp. 4 (A), 8 (A), 9, 12 (B), 20 (B), 23,
28 (A and B), 37, 40 (A), 43 (both), 46, 48 (A), 51 (E), 52 (B), 56 (A),
61, 63 (J and K), 64, 81 (left), 84 (A), 88 (A and B), 90 (D), 92 (A),
93 (D); Robert Harding Picture Library pp. 40 (B), 55 (G), 73; Palphot
Ltd. p. 45; Hutchison Library pp. 4 (B), 25, 35, 45 (B), 90 (E);
International Stock Exchange Photo Library p. 91 (H); ITC Entertainment
Ltd. pp. 8 (B), 12 (A and C), 16, 17, 20 (A), 28 (C), 44, 47, 48 (C),
52 (A), 56 (B), 60 (A and B), 67; Jewish Education Bureau p. 54 (E);
National Maritime Museum, Haifa (Israel) p. 91 (F); Network/Arkell p. 71
(top); Popperfoto p. 95 (I); David Richardson p. 53; Frank Spooner
Pictures/Basak p. 76 (A); Topham Picture Library p. 79; United Press
International p. 63 (I).

All other photographs supplied by the authors.

Cover photograph by Andes Press Agency/Carlos Reyes (painting by
Sister Marie S.M. and Paul Buckley of St. Mary of the Angels, Bayswater).

CONTENTS

Christians are people who believe that Jesus of Nazareth changed people's lives while he lived and that he goes on doing so now. So who was Jesus of Nazareth?

You can find out about the birth of Jesus by reading Matthew 1–2 and Luke 1–2 in the Christian Bible.

When Jesus was born in Judea, the country we now call Israel, it was ruled by the Roman Army. The Jews were expecting God to send a special person to help them. He was called 'the **Messiah**'. This means 'the **anointed** one'. Many Jews expected him to be a great fighter. They thought he would defeat the Romans and become their king.

Some Jews had read about the Messiah in their holy books. They knew that he would be a descendant of King David, and would be born in Bethlehem. A **prophet** called Isaiah said that a servant, the Messiah, would help people by healing them and by showing them the way God wanted them to behave. Isaiah also said the Messiah would suffer and die for his people.

JOSEPH'S STORY

Matthew 1–2 tells the story of the birth of Jesus from Joseph's point of view. One reason why God chose Joseph to be Jesus' father was because he was a descendant of King David. Joseph was told by God what Jesus was going to do on earth. His job was, 'to save His people from their sins'. He was also told to call the baby 'Jesus'. The name 'Jesus' means **'Saviour'**.

Matthew also tells us about the wise men visiting Jesus. They brought him three presents, so people think that there must have been three wise men. The wise men had come from the East. They followed a star. This led them to Bethlehem, where they found Jesus and his parents.

On the way to Bethlehem, they visited

A Inside the Church of the Nativity

B Outside the Church of the Nativity

C Bethlehem

King Herod. He lived in Jerusalem, which is only 6 km from Bethlehem. King Herod did not like them talking about a new king, so after the wise men had gone, he gave orders that all the baby boys in Bethlehem should be killed.

MARY'S STORY

You can read about Mary, Jesus' mother, in Luke 1–2. She was also a descendant of David. A messenger from God told her that her baby was going to be very special. She was told who Jesus was going to be. He was to be the 'Son of the Most High God'.

Luke tells us about the shepherds who came to visit Jesus. They were the first people to be told about the birth of this special baby.

D Painting of The Virgin Mary

WHEN DID THIS HAPPEN?

Luke was a very careful writer. He was interested in exact details such as dates. He tells us that all this happened when Augustus was the ruler of the Roman Empire, and Cyrenius was the governor of Syria. Matthew says that Herod the Great was the King of Judea. This makes it possible for us to date the birth of Jesus very accurately. It must have happened before Herod died in the year 4 BCE (Before the Common Era).

NOTES/DATABASE

Use the glossary to look up the meanings of the following words. Then use the definitions to make your own notes or suitable entries on your database.

Messiah	Prophet
Anointed	Saviour

ACTIVITIES

Make sure you have read Matthew 1:18–2:12 and Luke 1:1–2:20.

1 a Draw pictures of Mary and Joseph. Use the drawings above to help you.

Speech bubbles:
- Son of the Most High God
- God with us
- He shall save his people from their sins
- Jesus

b Place the correct speech bubbles next to Mary and Joseph to show what each of them was told about Jesus before he was born.

2 Copy and complete the following chart.

Questions	Matthew	Luke
a From whose point of view is the story told?		
b What is said about who Jesus will be?		
c Who came to see Jesus?		

FURTHER ACTIVITIES

BETHLEHEM STAR

SPECIAL CENSUS EDITION   **4 BCE**
SHEPHERDS REPORT STRANGE LIGHTS IN THE NIGHT SKY!

EXCLUSIVE!

Duty shepherds in the hills outside Bethlehem left their flocks last night after reporting strange happenings in the fields. They claim they were all wide awake. They had just finished their meal and were sitting by the fire when strange lights appeared in the sky as well as the sound of beautiful music. They admitted being scared stiff. The shepherds were joined by hundreds of people, who said they were messengers from God, telling them to hurry off to the local pub!

Apparently, the shepherds were told that the Messiah was born last night. They were told there would be a baby who had just been born in a cowshed behind the pub!

Our investigations have revealed that the baby is the son of a poor Galilean carpenter.

The shepherds have been charged with neglect of duty.

BIRTHS

Joseph and Mary announce the birth of their first son, who is to be called Joshua, or Jesus, which means 'Saviour'. They will return to Nazareth when Mary is fit to travel.

STOP PRESS!

There are now no free rooms to be found anywhere in Bethlehem. Members of the family of David, here for the census, are sleeping in the street.

Read the newspaper articles above.

Now answer these questions.

1 a Which parts of the story in the newspaper are the same as Luke 2:8–21? Which parts are different?

b Do you think that the writer of the newspaper report believed the shepherds? Write down reasons for your answer.

c In the Bible version of this event, what was the 'Good News' which the angels wanted the shepherds to know?

d Imagine that you lived in Bethlehem at the time when all this happened. Write a letter to the editor of the *Bethlehem Star*. Include your views about what happened that night.

You will need the following information when you complete the chart on page 7.

Mary and Joseph lived in Nazareth in Galilee. They had to go to Bethlehem because of the census. A census involves counting all the people in the country.

To get to Bethlehem, they had to go either through Samaria (Route A) or along the Jordan Valley to Jericho, then climb up the mountains and through the Judean Desert to Bethlehem (Route B).

The Jews and the Samaritans did not agree on religious matters. Many Jews would not travel through Samaria, or accept food or water from a Samaritan.

2 Copy the map into your book.

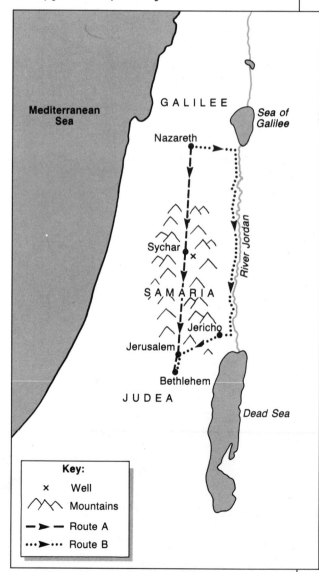

Key:

×	Well
/\/\/\	Mountains
– ► –	Route A
···►···	Route B

Routes from Nazareth to Bethlehem

3 Copy and complete the chart.

Question	Route A	Route B
a What kind of land would Mary and Joseph have had to cross?		
b Tick which route is the shortest.		
c Which countries would Mary and Joseph have had to cross?		
d Where could Mary and Joseph find drinking water?		
e Where would Mary and Joseph find somewhere to stay?		
f Tick the route you think Mary and Joseph would have chosen.		

Did you know?
The name Bethlehem means 'House of Bread'. Later on Jesus called himself the 'Bread of Life'.

4 For your notes/database

Augustus Caesar 27 BCE – 14 CE Emperor of Rome when Jesus was born.

Herod the Great 75 BCE – 4 BCE Great builder and statesman, King of Judea when Jesus was born.

Cyrenius Roman Governor of Syria for a short while at the time when Jesus was born.

5 Answer these questions in complete sentences

a If you were told that a king had been born, where would you expect to find him?

b Where did the wise men expect to find Jesus?

c What was the reason for Mary and Joseph going to Bethlehem?

d Explain how we can work out the year in which Jesus was born.

A star led the wise men to Jesus. The Star of David, sometimes known as the Star of Bethlehem, is the symbol of the Jewish people.

Martin Luther, a sixteenth century German Christian, went for a walk in the forest in 1521. He saw a fir tree surrounded by stars, twinkling in the evening sky. It reminded him that Jesus came from heaven to be the Light of the World. He went home, and set up the first Christmas tree in his house.

6 a Draw a picture of a star and of a Christmas tree.

b How does a star help to remind Christians of the birth of Jesus?

c How can a Christmas tree help to remind Christians about who Jesus really is?

WAITING FOR THE MESSIAH

In the time of Jesus the Jews were waiting for God to send a Messiah – a special person – to be their leader. He would show them how God wanted them to behave. Some Jews thought he would be a fighter who would free them from the Romans.

In the time of Jesus there was a man called John the Baptist. Many people from Jerusalem and the surrounding area walked long distances into the desert to hear him speak about God.

Some people thought that John was the Messiah. John said that he was not, but that he was a messenger who God had sent on ahead to tell people to expect the Messiah at any moment. His job was to help people to get ready for the Messiah. Look at the Isaiah scroll.

PREACHER IN THE DESERT

John lived in the desert, quite near to the town of Jericho and to the Dead Sea. People from Jerusalem came to hear him

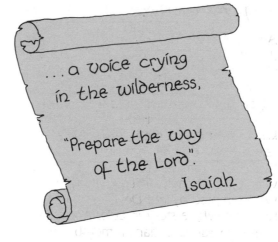

...a voice crying in the wilderness,

"Prepare the way of the Lord".

Isaiah

preach. You can find out the kind of things which he told people to do, by reading Luke 3:7–14.

John lived in the desert. He wore desert clothes – camel skins – instead of the usual wool or linen clothes which most people wore. He ate the kind of food which he could find in the desert – locusts and wild honey.

John thought it very important that people should treat each other honestly and fairly and try to help one another. Sometimes, he wasn't very polite to the people who had come to hear him preach. He once called them a 'family of snakes'!

John thought that people needed to change their lifestyle and to behave the way God wanted them to. He thought they needed to do something special as a sign that they wanted to change, so he asked people to be **'baptized'**. To do this he took them into the River Jordan, and ducked them under the water as a sign that they had given up doing wrong things and wanted to spend the rest of their lives living in the way God wanted.

John said, 'I baptize you with water, but one day, someone is going to come, who will baptize you with the **Holy Spirit** instead'. John thought that he wouldn't be good enough even to untie that person's shoelaces!

A Judean Desert

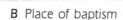
B Place of baptism

JESUS IS BAPTIZED

One day, Jesus came to John and asked to be baptized. Immediately John knew that this was the special person sent by God to be the Messiah. He didn't want to baptize Jesus, but Jesus insisted and so he was baptized by John in the River Jordan, in the same way as thousands of other people.

When Jesus came up out of the water, John was sure that he was right. This was the Messiah! A cloud came near them, and a dove appeared in the cloud, and they heard a voice which said, 'This is my son, I love him, and I am pleased with him'.

SIGNS THAT GOD IS REAL

In the Old Testament, the cloud is always a sign of the presence of God. It was a cloud which led the Israelites out of Egypt and into the promised land, and a cloud which hung over the holiest place in the Temple. The dove showed that God was with them in a special way, through His Holy Spirit.

TEMPTATION

After Jesus was baptized, he went into the desert for a long time. During that time he thought about, and worked out what it meant to have this special relationship with God, and how God wanted him to use it to help people to know God and serve God better. He rejected some ways in which he might have been tempted to use his relationship with God wrongly. The Bible says he was 'tempted by the Devil'. You can read the whole story in Luke 4:1–13.

Every year, Christians remember this part of Jesus' life during Lent, which is the forty days leading up to the great festival of Easter.

NOTES/DATABASE

Use the glossary to look up the meanings of the following words. Then use the definitions to make your own notes or suitable entries on your database.

Baptized	Disciple
Holy Spirit	Christian
Essenes	

C Mount of Temptation at Jericho

ACTIVITIES

1 Read about John the Baptist in Luke 3:1–20.

Now answer these questions.

a Look at verse 3. What was the most important part of John's preaching?

b Copy and complete the chart.

In column A, write down the name of the group of people who asked John for advice.

In column B write down the advice he gave them.

A Who asked John for advice?	**B** What advice did he give them?

2 Read Mark 1:1–12.

a Some people thought John might have been the Messiah. Why do you think they thought this?

b What did John say about the 'person coming after' him?

3 a John said there was a difference between the way he baptized people, and the way the Messiah would baptize them. Using verse 8, write a sentence which explains what that difference is.

b Where did Jesus come from when he came to be baptized?

c How did Jesus know that God was pleased with him?

d Immediately after his baptism, where did Jesus go?

FURTHER ACTIVITIES

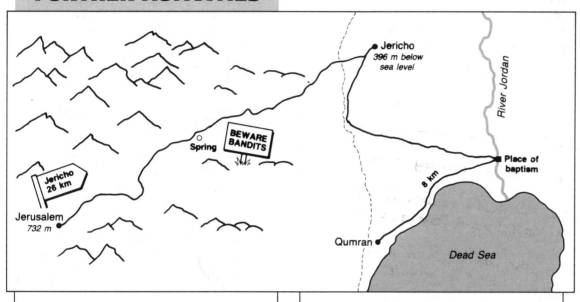

1 Look at the map.

This map shows you the route from Jerusalem to Jericho which people would have had to follow if they had wanted to go to hear John preach.

a People walk at the rate of about 5 km per hour. How long would it have taken them to get from Jerusalem to the place where John was preaching?

b Why do you think it might have taken them a lot longer to get home again?

c What reasons do you think people might have had for going on a difficult journey to see and hear John the Baptist?

2 Look at the map again.

Some people think that John the Baptist may have been a member of a group of men who lived at Qumran, called the **Essenes**. (Find Qumran on your map.) They wrote the Dead Sea Scrolls. These were a library of scrolls containing information about their way of life, as well as some copies of parts of the Old Testament. They were found hidden in a cave near Qumran. The Essenes taught people to live honest lives, caring about other people, in preparation for the time when the Messiah would come. They also baptized new members, as well as insisting on washing as a sign of purity.

a How far is it from Qumran to the place where John baptized people?

b Write down **two** ways in which John the Baptist was similar to the people who lived at Qumran.

THOUSANDS FLOCK TO HEAR DESERT PREACHER!

People are leaving Jerusalem in their thousands, and flocking out to hear a desert preacher.

Has the voice of prophecy returned to Israel?

For 400 years the voice of prophecy has been silent in Israel. Until now! Has God visited his people yet again? In the last few weeks a new prophet has been preaching in the desert near Jericho. His name is John bar Zechariah, and if his name seems familiar, it is because his father, may he rest in peace, was a much respected priest in the temple here in Jerusalem.

Zechariah would scarcely have approved of this wild son of his who dresses in old camel skins, and lives on locusts!

However, his message is very much the same as that of the prophets of the past. 'Turn back to God', he says, 'Treat your fellow men the way you would want them to behave towards you'. There is nothing new in the message. What is new is the demand that Jews should show the change in their lives by being baptized, a practice until now reserved for Gentile women wanting to become believers in the God of Israel.

D The cave where the Dead Sea scrolls were found

3 Read the newspaper cutting and the letter from Andrew about the prophet John.

Imagine that you have been to the desert to hear John preach. Write your own letter to a friend about your visit to John. Make sure that you have read pages 8 and 9 to help you do this.

To Simon the Fisherman,
Capernaum,
Galilee,
Israel.

Dear Simon,
 Have you heard about this new prophet? Everyone here in Jerusalem is absolutely over the moon with him!
 Last Sabbath (Yes, I know we shouldn't walk more than 2000 paces on the Sabbath) James and I went out into the Judean desert to hear him preach. Scores of people were pouring out of Jerusalem, all to listen to John.
 I was exhausted when we got there! Well, you know what the road to Jericho is like — 26 km of dust and rock — only one spring on the way — all downhill, and no shade! At least it was better than the climb back up to Jerusalem!
 When we got there, this prophet was dressed in Camel skins. Well, well, I ask you, did you ever see a decent looking Camel skin, when the Camel was still using it, let alone when he'd finished with it! Apparently, the fellow lives on locusts and wild honey!
 When we got there, he wasn't even polite — he called us a collection of snakes!
 However, Simon, I think you must try to get down there to hear him. I have my suspicions that he might actually be the Messiah we are all waiting for.
                    Come Soon,
                     Love,
                      Andrew!

The Messiah?

A Prophet?

Elijah come again?

BAPTISM NOW

Jesus' **disciples** (his followers) went on baptizing people. Later on, **Christians** baptized new members to show that they believed in Jesus and wanted to follow him. Christians now are often baptized. Some babies are baptized because their Christian parents want their children to receive the sign of belonging to Jesus too. Other Christians believe that it is better to wait until people believe in Jesus for themselves, and want to promise to follow him for the rest of their lives.

4 Sue and James are a young Christian couple who have just had a baby. What reasons do you think they might give for choosing to have their baby baptized?

5 Leroy is a teenage Christian who attends a Baptist church. He has just decided that he wants to be baptized. What reasons do you think he might have had for making this decision?

'I accept the Lord Jesus Christ as my personal saviour.'

JESUS' FIRST DISCIPLES

Soon after Jesus was baptized, he began to choose some people to follow him. They needed to learn many things about Jesus himself, and about the Kingdom of God.

Jesus chose ordinary people, who had ordinary jobs, to follow him. We usually call these people **'disciples'**. This means 'pupils' or people who are learning.

Jesus had many followers. Men and women followed him all around Israel. In those days there were many wandering Jewish religious leaders who had a band of followers who went everywhere with them to learn about God.

Jesus chose twelve people to be his special friends. He taught them about himself, and God the Father, and about the Kingdom of God. You can find a list of all twelve disciples in Mark 3:13–19.

The first people to become his followers were fishermen, from Capernaum in Galilee. They were fishing when Jesus asked them to come with him. They were ready to leave their fishing immediately to go with Jesus.

A Galilee at Tiberias today

Their names were Simon, Andrew, James and John. They remained Jesus' closest friends. (Read the story of how they first followed Jesus in Luke 5:1–11.)

Another person from Galilee who followed Jesus was Levi, or Matthew, who was a **tax collector**. (Find the story in Mark 2:13–17). Jews did not like tax collectors because many of them were dishonest, and because they worked for the Romans. They were treated as traitors. Many **Jews** refused to

B The first followers were fishermen

eat with tax collectors. Jesus was often criticized for mixing with people like tax collectors, and for being ready to eat with them as well.

THE WORK OF A DISCIPLE

C Followers of Jesus

Sometimes, Jesus sent his disciples out in pairs to teach people, and to heal their illnesses. He gave them careful instructions. They were told to be like the other very poor people, and not carry lots of possessions with them. If someone offered them a bed for the night, they were to accept, but if they were not welcomed, then they should go somewhere else (Mark 6:6–12). When the time came for Jesus to leave his disciples he told them that their job was only just beginning. They were instructed by Jesus to go everywhere in the world to tell people about him (Matthew 28:19).

Soon, the first disciples, and other people who believed in Jesus, were given a special relationship with God to help them to tell the rest of the world about Jesus. They went all over the Roman Empire telling people that everyone could be friends with God and know that God was with them all the time.

FOLLOWING JESUS NOW

Today, disciples of Jesus are still doing the same thing. They want to tell other people about Jesus, and help them to believe in him too. Some people leave their own homes to follow Jesus, just as the first disciples did. Often, they have to learn new languages, and have to live a different kind of life. Sometimes, like the first disciples, they have to face dangers when they tell others about Jesus, and some of them have even died. In spite of this, Christians go on doing what Jesus asked his followers to do, that is, telling the whole world about him.

D A Salvation Army band

NOTES/DATABASE

Use the glossary to look up the meanings of the following words. Then use the definitions to make your own notes or suitable entries on your database.

Disciple   Jew

Tax collector

COME WITH ME!

Jesus was walking by the lakeside when he saw Simon and Andrew in their boat. He called to them and told them to come and follow him.

Later on, he passed James and John, who were also fishermen, and he asked them to come with him too.

Now read Mark 1:16–20.

1 Draw pictures of Jesus talking to Simon and Andrew, and then to James and John.

Write what you think they might have said to each other in speech bubbles. Use the pictures below to help you.

One afternoon, Jesus was walking by the Lake of Galilee when . . .

he saw Simon and Andrew fishing.

Later on . . .

he saw James and John.

FURTHER ACTIVITIES

1 Look at the list of the names of the twelve disciples in Mark 3:13–19.

WANTED

TWELVE MEN TO CHANGE THE WORLD

Must be prepared to leave home and family in search of new challenges.

Suitable applicants will be hard working and self-motivated, interested in travelling and meeting new people.

REWARD: The Kingdom of God!

Apply in person to:

JESUS OF NAZARETH
of
No Fixed Abode.

No qualifications or previous experience necessary

Imagine you are one of the disciples. Now write a letter applying for a position as one of Jesus' disciples.

THE COST OF FOLLOWING JESUS

2 Read Luke 9:57–62.

The table has three conversations between Jesus and people who wanted to follow him.

Copy and complete the table. You will find the correct verse listed in column A. You will need to write Jesus' reply in column C.

A Verse	B Person	C Jesus' reply
a 57	I will follow you wherever you go.	
b 59	Let me first go and bury my father.	
c 61	Let me go and say goodbye to my family.	

Simon the fisherman was later given another name by Jesus. He was called Peter. Don't be confused by the names — it's the same person. He was even called Simon Peter sometimes.

Peter was already married when he met Jesus. One day, Jesus went home to his house for a meal, and healed Peter's mother-in-law who was ill.

When you find the truth, by Jimmy and Carol Owens.

Peter's wife

When I wore my bridal veil and wedding gown
I said my vows and dreamed of how we'd settle down:
Of course I thought my husband ought to stick around,
But now it seems that the man of my dreams is always out of town!

Well, I guess I married a travellin' man.
But I've met Jesus so I understand
That when you find the truth, you'll follow Him anywhere,
When you find the truth you'll follow Him anywhere.

I thought he'd come straight home from fishing ev'ry day,
But sometimes the way of God is not a woman's way:
My mother rolls her eyes and softly sighs, 'Oyvey!'
And wonders how I'll be able to smile each time he goes away!

Well, I guess I married a travellin' man,
But I've met Jesus so I understand
That when you find the truth you'll follow Him anywhere,
When you find the truth you'll follow Him anywhere!

3 Read the words of the song, 'When you find the truth'. Now answer these questions.

  a How do you think Peter's wife felt about her husband following Jesus around the country? Did knowing Jesus help her to understand?

  b Many children whose parents are missionaries are left behind at school or with grandparents. If this happened to you, how would you feel about it? Would you find it difficult to understand the importance of their work?

Did you know?
In Jesus' time, people didn't have surnames. Instead the son of Zebedee would have been called bar Zebedee.

Cor! That means that if I had lived in Jesus' time I would have been called John bar Bill, and my brother James bar Bill.

TOP SECRET
NAME: James bar Zebedee
NEXT OF KIN: Father, Zebedee
FAMILY CONNECTIONS: Brother, John, possibly twins
DATE OF BIRTH: Unknown, thought to be about 10 CE
PLACE OF BIRTH: Possibly Capernaum, Galilee
OCCUPATION: Fisherman
ADDRESS: Currently, no fixed abode
PREVIOUS ADDRESS: (if different from above)
12, Fisherman's Terrace,
Capernaum,
Galilee,
Israel.
MARITAL STATUS: Single
CHILDREN: None
POLITICS: Little known, but thought to be anti-Roman Jewish Nationalist
RELIGIOUS AFFILIATION: Follower of wandering Rabbi, Jesus of Nazareth
OTHER DETAILS: James and his brother John were among the first followers of Jesus of Nazareth (who was later executed by the Romans). Originally a fisherman, James became one of Jesus' closest friends.

He was said to have been present when Jesus raised a little girl, the daughter of synagogue leader Jairus from the dead.

On another occasion, James claimed to have been with Jesus, John and another fisherman friend from Capernaum named Simon, when they all had a vision of Moses and Elijah.

Executed for continuing to believe Jesus was alive, shortly after the Crucifixion of Jesus, about 28 CE.

4 Work out what you would have been called.

Group work
5 Form a group of 4–6 people. First of all, use Mark 3:13–19 to make a list of the names of all twelve disciples.

  Now use a Bible dictionary, or a Bible names database, to find out as much as you can about each of the disciples.

  Look at the form above which tells you James' personal details. Draw your own pictures of each of the other disciples. Design and fill in a form for each disciple like the one above.

TEACHING BY EXAMPLE

Jesus taught people by the way he treated others, as well as by what he said. 'You have seen the way the Kings of the **Gentiles** come among you', he said, 'but I come like a servant'. He said his followers should behave in the same way (Luke 22:25). The really important person is the one who is prepared to be the servant.

During supper, on the night before he died, Jesus took a towel, wrapped it round himself, and knelt down on the floor to wash his disciples' feet. He was teaching his disciples that their job was to serve other people. It was easier for them to learn this lesson through seeing Jesus behave like a servant, than by him simply telling them (John 13:1–20).

EVERYDAY THINGS

Jesus wanted ordinary people to hear and to understand his teaching. It wasn't just intended for very clever or well-educated people. He taught them by using examples from the everyday things which they saw around them, and which they all knew about. For example, if you read Mark 4 you will find some examples of how Jesus used the idea of plants growing, to show people what the **Kingdom of God** was like. This kind of story with an extra meaning is called a **parable**.

Wherever Jesus went, all over Israel, many people wanted to hear him teach The way he taught them about God, and the way God wanted them to behave, was new and exciting. Other religious teachers at the time, called **scribes** and **Pharisees**, told them about all the rules they had to keep to please God. Jesus showed people that it was important to treat each other with love and respect. This was what God really wanted. The ordinary people were amazed at the way he taught. They said he spoke 'with authority'.

LOOK AROUND YOU!

One day, John the Baptist's disciples came to see Jesus. They asked whether Jesus was the Messiah. He didn't say yes or no. Instead, he said, 'Look around you and see what is happening, people are being healed . . . and the poor are hearing the good news'. (Find the whole story in Luke 7:18–23.) It was important to Jesus that ordinary people should understand his teaching.

Jesus often referred to his message about the Kingdom of God as 'the good news'. The old word for this was 'gospel'. The good news which he came to bring was not just for Jews or very religious people, but for everyone. By believing and trusting in Jesus, they could all have a special relationship with God. Jesus taught everyone to call God 'Father', and to realize that God loved each one of them, and was concerned about every detail of their lives.

Sometimes Jesus taught the people by speaking to many of them at once. On one occasion, he was teaching people on the beach at Capernaum. There were so many people crowding round, wanting to listen, that he had to climb into Simon Peter's boat to avoid getting his feet wet! (Luke 5:1–11).

A Fishermen on the beach at Tiberius

In Matthew 5, you can find a collection of some of the things which Jesus said. He always seemed to encourage the poor and ordinary people. He was always interested in those no-one else had any time for. Read Matthew 5:3–10, and you will see how Jesus tried to encourage anyone who might be unhappy.

Jesus' whole life was a message. Through his life, death and **resurrection** (coming back to life again), he taught everyone to love both God and other people.

B The Sermon on the Mount

NOTES/DATABASE

Use the glossary to look up the meanings of the following words. Then use the definitions to make your own notes or suitable entries on your database.

Gentile	Scribe
Kingdom of God	Pharisee
Parable	Resurrection

ACTIVITIES

HOW JESUS TAUGHT PEOPLE

1 Copy and complete the following chart.

In column A you will find one of the ways in which Jesus taught people. Use the information on these pages to find an example of this method of teaching, and enter the Bible reference for this method of teaching in column B, and the example you have found in column C.

A Method	B Bible reference	C Example
a by example		
b in parables		
c by telling them things		

2 Answer these questions. Read this unit to help you think about the answers.

   a When Jesus washed the disciples' feet, what do you think he was trying to teach them?

   b What did Jesus mean by good news?

   c Write down **two** ways in which Jesus taught so that ordinary people could understand his teaching.

   d How did Jesus answer John's disciples when they came and asked him whether he was the Messiah or not?

   e Do you think he was actually saying yes or no in his reply to John's disciples?

3 Read Matthew 5:3–10.

Write in column B the reason why the group of people listed in column A may think of themselves as blessed (happy in the Good News Bible).

A Group of people	B Why they are blessed
a The poor	
b Mourners	
c Humble people	
d Those who want to do what God wants	
e Those who show mercy to other people	
f The pure in heart	
g Those who work for peace	

JESUS THE TEACHER

FURTHER ACTIVITIES

PARABLES

1 Read Luke 15.

There are three stories in this chapter which Jesus told about how God loves and cares about people who are wandering away from the way God wants them to live.

The lost sheep. Read the story, then match the correct labels to the pictures (Luke 15:1–7).

GOTCHA!

99,100, Yes, all there!

WHERE'S FRED? HE'S ALWAYS WANDERING OFF

LOOK FOLKS I'VE FOUND FRED

LOVE ONE ANOTHER

Jesus wanted his followers to love one another.

One day, someone asked Jesus what the most important law was. Find out what Jesus said by reading Luke 10:25–28.

Now read on! (Luke 10:29–37).

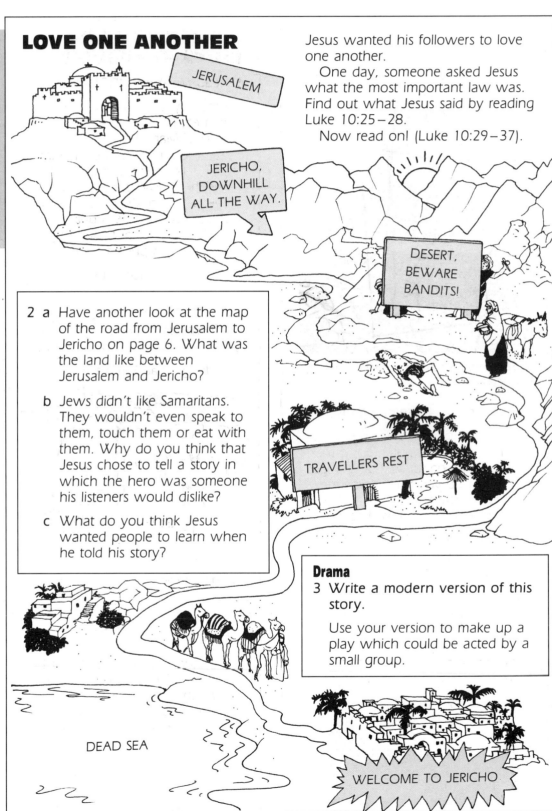

JERUSALEM

JERICHO, DOWNHILL ALL THE WAY.

DESERT, BEWARE BANDITS!

TRAVELLERS REST

DEAD SEA

WELCOME TO JERICHO

2 a Have another look at the map of the road from Jerusalem to Jericho on page 6. What was the land like between Jerusalem and Jericho?

b Jews didn't like Samaritans. They wouldn't even speak to them, touch them or eat with them. Why do you think that Jesus chose to tell a story in which the hero was someone his listeners would dislike?

c What do you think Jesus wanted people to learn when he told his story?

Drama

3 Write a modern version of this story.

Use your version to make up a play which could be acted by a small group.

4 Luke 15:9–10

The coins in this story are from a bride's head-dress. Read the story.

C Yemenite Jewish bride with coins in her head-dress.

Now answer these questions.

a To lose one of these coins was like someone today losing their engagement or wedding ring. What do you think someone now would do if they lost their engagement or wedding ring?

b What do you think the woman in the story did when she found her coin?

c What do you think Jesus was trying to tell people about God when he told this story?

5 Luke 15:11–32.

The lost son. Read the story.
Now draw a series of cartoons which retell the story. If you want to, you could bring this story up to date, and retell it as if it was happening now.

WHO IS PART OF GOD'S KINGDOM?

6 Read Matthew 25:31–46.

One day, Jesus told a story about himself. In it he called himself the 'Son of Man'. He said that one day, he will divide people into two sets, in the same way as a shepherd divides his flock into sheep and goats. He tells us, in the story, how he is going to decide who to put on his right, and who to put on his left.

Copy the picture below.

Read the story again, and then write in each of the folds (the places where the shepherds keep their animals) what people in each set have done to be placed in that set.

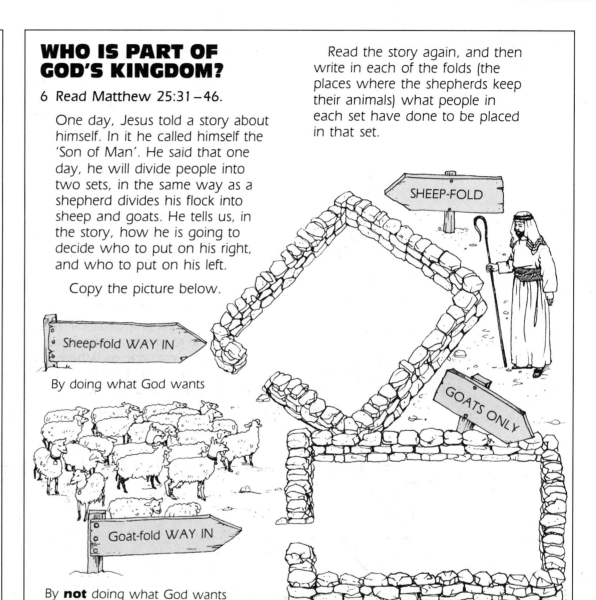

Sheep-fold WAY IN

By doing what God wants

Goat-fold WAY IN

By **not** doing what God wants

SHEEP-FOLD

GOATS ONLY

7 a Ian knows the Bible very well, and goes to church every Sunday. A new boy has just moved in next door, and is feeling very lonely. However, Ian is too busy with church activities to make friends with him. Is this what God wants? Write down some reasons for your answer.

b Sarah doesn't go to church. Instead, she spends a lot of time trying to help Jane, whose husband is in prison. Jane has four young children, and very little money. She finds life difficult. Sarah helps whenever she can. Is Sarah doing what God wants? Write down some reasons for your answer.

Jesus was full of God's power. During his **ministry** (this is what we call the time when he was showing the world who he was, and telling them about God), he used his power to help other people.

HEALING THE SICK

Sometimes, he used his power to explain something more about who he was. For example, once four men brought a man who couldn't walk to see Jesus. They couldn't get into the house, because it was crowded with people who were listening to Jesus. They decided to climb up onto the flat roof. They made a hole

A Jesus preaching in the synagogue

in the roof big enough to let the man down through it. When Jesus saw the man, he said, 'Your sins are forgiven'. People were very surprised because they knew that only God had the power to forgive sins. Jesus said that he would heal the man to prove that he really had the power to forgive sins. He was claiming to be equal with God (Mark 2:1–12).

When Jesus began to show the world who he was, he went to the **synagogue** and was asked to read from the **Scriptures**, and to tell the people what they meant. Jesus chose a section of the prophet Isaiah, which said that the Messiah would make blind people see, deaf people hear, and lame people walk, and tell poor people the good news that God loves them. He told them that this **prophecy** had come true today (Luke 4:18–21).

Jesus did exactly what this prophecy said. He made blind people see (Matthew 9:27–31), deaf people hear (Mark 7:31–37), and lame people walk (Mark 2:1–12). All these, and many

B Ruins of the synagogue at Capernaum

other **miracles** of healing, helped people to believe that he was the Messiah.

FEEDING THE HUNGRY

There were other kinds of miracles. All four **Gospels** tell us how Jesus felt sorry for a great crowd of people who had followed him all day, and were getting hungry. One of his disciples found that a little boy had five bread rolls and two small fish. He gave these to Jesus, who blessed them, and broke them into pieces in the usual Jewish way. There was then enough bread and fish to feed five thousand people, and some left over (John 6:35–44).

This miracle was important because it reminded people of the time when God had fed the people of Israel in the wilderness (Exodus 16). This also helped people believe that Jesus was someone special.

RAISING THE DEAD

Jesus had a special friend who lived near Jerusalem, called Lazarus. When Lazarus was sick, everyone thought that Jesus would rush to Bethany, where he lived, to heal him. Jesus did not go there until three days after Lazarus had died. Even then, Lazarus' sisters believed that Jesus could help. They trusted in Jesus, and knew that Jesus was God's son. They believed that he could raise Lazarus from the dead. 'I am the **Resurrection** and the life', said Jesus. Lazarus was already buried in a tomb, but he came alive again. This helped people believe that Jesus was the Messiah, and also prepared them for Jesus' own resurrection from the dead.

Jesus never used miracles to help himself. On the Cross, he was challenged to save himself but he left God to do the greater miracle of raising his son from the dead. This helped people to understand that through Jesus, everyone can have a new kind of life as God's friend.

NOTES/DATABASE

Use the glossary to look up the meanings of the following words. Then use the definitions to make your own notes or suitable entries on your database.

Ministry	Prophecy
Synagogue	Gospels
Scriptures	Miracle
Prophet	Resurrection

ACTIVITIES

1 Answer in complete sentences.

a Did Jesus use his power
  i to help himself
  ii to help other people?

b Read the story of the man who was let down through the roof in Mark 2:1–12. Imagine you were in the room listening to Jesus. Write your account of what happened that day.

c How did Jesus use his miracles to show that Isaiah's prophecy about the Messiah (Luke 4:18–21) had come true?

d Why was the feeding of the five thousand important to the Jews?

e Read John 11 to find out more about Lazarus and his two sisters. Why do you think Jesus waited so long before he went to see his friend?

f Jesus could work miracles. What reasons can you think of for Jesus choosing not to work a miracle to save himself from dying on the Cross?

WHERE TO FIND JESUS' MIRACLES OF HEALING

Miracles of healing	Matthew	Mark	Luke	John
Man with skin disease	8:2–3	1:40–42	5:12–13	
Roman soldier's servant	8:5–13		7:1–10	
Peter's mother-in-law	8:14f	1:30f	4:38f	
Two men from Gadara	8:28–34	5:1–15	8:27–35	
Paralysed man	9:2–7	2:3–12	5:18–26	
Woman with haemorrhage	9:20–22	5:25–29	8:43–48	
Two blind men	9:27–31			
Man dumb and possessed	9:32f			
Man with paralysed hand	12:10–13	3:1–5	6:6–10	
Man blind, dumb, possessed	12:22			
Foreign woman's daughter	15:21–28	7:24–30		
Epileptic boy	17:14–18	9:17–29	9:38–43	
Two blind men	20:29–34			
Bartimaeus		10:46–52	18:35–43	
Deaf mute		7:31–37		
Possessed man (synagogue)		1:23–26	4:33–35	
Blind man at Bethsaida		8:22–26		
Crippled woman			13:11–13	
Man with swollen limbs			14:1–14	
Ten lepers			17:10–19	
High priest's servant			22:50f	
Official's son				4:46–54
Man at pool				5:1–19
Man at pool				9

What does the letter f mean?

It means read that verse and the next one!

2 a Copy and complete the table shown here. When completed this is a bar chart of Jesus' miracles. Write the rest of the Bible references in Matthew for each section.

b Do the same thing for Mark.

c Now repeat this for Luke.

Matthew 9:27–31	Matthew 9:1–8	Matthew 9:32f	Matthew 8:2–3
Blind	Lame	Deaf	Others

THE POWER OF JESUS

FURTHER ACTIVITIES

Read the extracts from Peter's diary. They are based on events which are recorded in John's Gospel.
Diary entry A is based on John 2:1–12.
Diary entry B is based on John 4:46–54.

A — THE FIRST DAY — DIARY — 25 C.E.

Went with Jesus to a wedding at Cana. They ran out of wine. Jesus' mum told him about it and he said "It's not the right time yet". – She told the servants to do whatever he told them. He made them go and fill the water pots (6 of them each holding 100 litres) with water. – They were exhausted. Then Jesus made someone put the water in a wine glass – and when they all tasted it, it wasn't water it was wine!
Who is this man? Certainly not an ordinary carpenter!
Very late when we got back to Capernaum. Jesus stayed the night.

B — SOME TIME LATER — DIARY — 25 C.E.

Can't keep up with this Jesus. We're always rushing around. Just got back from Jerusalem, and now we've come back to Cana – don't even have chance to talk to the wife at Capernaum!
Extraordinary thing happened! The son of this fellow from the government who lives in the big house in Capernaum was dying – so the fellow walked all the way to Cana (25 miles) to ask Jesus to heal the boy. Well, Jesus wouldn't go back to Capernaum – but told the fellow his son was better already! "Go back home, your son will live," he said.
Anyway, I can't wait to get back to Capernaum to find out what happened.

1 Read John 2:1–12.

Imagine you were one of the guests at the wedding at Cana. Write your own diary entry, saying what happened when they ran out of wine.

2 Read John 4:46–54.

Draw a series of cartoons to explain what happened. Make sure you put captions under each picture, and use speech bubbles so that the story is easy to understand.

ONCE I WAS BLIND, BUT NOW I CAN SEE

You will need to use John 9 to help you to find the answers to these puzzles and questions.

One day, Jesus and his disciples met a blind man.

Blind from birth

Spare a penny for a poor blind beggar

3 a Describe the story shown in the drawings, and include what would have been said in the empty speech bubbles. Use verses 1–3 to help you.

b What did Jesus do?

c What did Jesus ask the blind man to do?

d Copy and complete the following sentences using verses 8–24 to help you.

When the blind man returned, he could ....

He was taken to the ....

They were furious because Jesus healed the man on the ....

They thought Jesus must be a ....

e What did the man say about Jesus? (verse 17).

f Read verses 18–23. Write down what the Pharisees and the blind man's parents said.

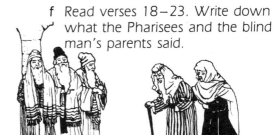

The Pharisees said . . .   His parents said . . .

g Copy and complete these sentences.

First the man said (verse 11) 'He is a ....'

Then (verse 17), 'He is a ....'

Later, he said (verse 33) '.............. ....'

Finally (verse 38) the man said to Jesus '.. ....'

GOD'S HEALING POWER IN ACTION!

Christians believe that God miraculously heals people today, through prayer. Although God has the power to heal wherever they are, many people believe that some places are specially chosen by God, as Holy places where he has chosen to heal people. Roman Catholic Christians believe that God often chooses to heal people in Lourdes, a small town in Southern France.

A French peasant girl, called Bernadette Soubirous, was playing one day in a cave near the river called 'The Grotto of Marsebeilles', when a lady wearing a white dress appeared to her. She said that she was Mary, the mother of Jesus, and that she wanted a church built

there. A stream appeared on that spot, and the lady said that it would have healing powers.

Ever since then, thousands of people go to Lourdes to pray and to worship God there. Many of them also ask God for healing. There are many cases, recorded by doctors there, of people being healed, without the use of medicine.

C Lourdes where many people go to be healed

4 Discuss the answers to these questions in a small group before writing down your own individual answers.

a Why do you think that Christians have gone on believing that God can heal people?

b Do you think that going to a special place like Lourdes helps people to pray for healing?

c What other reasons do you think someone might have for going to Lourdes?

Something to do

Ask your local Roman Catholic Church for information about ACROSS and the JUMBULANCE. It might be possible to arrange for the JUMBULANCE to visit your school.

Quite often, Jesus disagreed with the Jewish authorities. **Pharisees** believed it was important to keep the **Jewish Religious Law** in all its exact details. If all the people of Israel kept the whole of the law for the whole of the day, then they believed the **Messiah** would come.

THE SABBATH

For many people, keeping the **Sabbath** (Holy day) had become a difficulty instead of a joy. Like the **prophets** of the Old Testament, Jesus thought it was more important to stick to what the law actually meant, rather than minute details. By the time of Jesus, lots of extra laws had been added. Many of these concerned the Sabbath.

In the Ten **Commandments** there was only one law about the Sabbath, 'Remember the Sabbath and keep it Holy'.

The Sabbath was the seventh day. It was a day on which no one should do any work. Carrying things, cooking, walking more than 2000 paces were all against the rules.

PICKING CORN

In Mark 2:23–37, Jesus and his disciples got into trouble for working on the Sabbath . . . they were getting the middle out of some ears of corn to eat it, while strolling through the fields! When they were criticized, Jesus replied, 'The Sabbath was made for the good of man, not man for the Sabbath'.

Later that day, a man with a withered hand was in the **synagogue**. They wanted to see what Jesus would do. He healed the man. (Mark 3:1–6.) Jesus believed that it was right to do good and help people even on the Sabbath.

On another occasion, Jesus was in Jerusalem when he met a man who had been crippled for thirty-eight years. Jesus healed the man, and told him to pick up his bed and carry it back home. Unfortunately, the man got caught by the religious authorities who told him,

START HERE!

586 BCE
Jews exiled to Babylon

BABYLON A VERY LONG WAY

Jerusalem left in ruins

'How can we go on being Jews in a strange land?'

So they decided to live Holy lives, and read the Bible carefully, adding helpful bits of rules to make them better Jews.

70 YEARS LATER!

JERUSALEM, A VERY LONG WAY BACK

King of Babylon

'You can go back to Jerusalem!'

'Great, we can rebuild the Temple and be real Jews again!'

But some Jews stayed in Babylon . . . they all needed the new rules to help them be better Jews.

THEN!

POW!

CONQUERED BY GREEKS!

'What a nerve, putting their idols in our Temple!'

'Good job we've got those rules to help us to be good Jews!'

CRASH!

POW!

'Oh no! not again!'

'It's the Romans this time, with their pagan gods!'

So, by the time of Jesus, the Religious Law was very important. It held Jewish life together, and stopped them being swamped by other nations.

'This is the Sabbath!' The authorities began to persecute Jesus, not because he healed people, but because he did it every day, including the Sabbath. They thought God did not want people to do any work on the Sabbath.

The Pharisees were honestly trying to serve God as they thought right. That is why they were so upset when they saw Jesus doing something which they thought to be wrong. They were even more upset when they found Jesus claiming to be equal with God.

CLAIMING TO BE EQUAL WITH GOD

When Jesus healed the paralysed man (Mark 2:1–12), he said to the man, 'Your sins are forgiven'. The Pharisees were good Jews. They knew that only God could forgive sins. Each day, they said in their prayers, 'The Lord our God is one'. Their belief in the one God who forgives sins made it difficult for them to accept that Jesus could even say 'Your sins are forgiven'. They thought that this was blasphemy, or speaking against God. They understood that this was a claim, by Jesus, to be God Himself.

So, the two reasons why the religious authorities decided to execute Jesus were: **a** because they thought he worked on the Sabbath, and **b** because he claimed to be equal with God.

NOTES/DATABASE

Use the glossary to look up the meanings of the following words. Then use the definitions to make your own notes or suitable entries on your database.

Pharisees	Prophet
Jewish Religious Law	Commandments
	Synagogue
Messiah	
Sabbath	

ACTIVITIES

1 a When did many Jews think the Messiah would come?

   b List **three** things which were against the law on the Sabbath.

   c Why did the Pharisees object to Jesus healing someone on the Sabbath?

   d Why did the Pharisees object to Jesus saying, 'Your sins are forgiven'?

SABBATH LAWS

The Sabbath laws were intended to help people spend time worshipping God. Even the woman of the household had a day off on the Sabbath. She was not allowed to cook meals . . . this was working.

Animals were looked after, but they were not allowed to work either, so a donkey was not expected to carry his master around on the Sabbath.

Sabbath began when there were three stars in the sky on Friday evening. It ended when three stars appeared in the sky on Saturday evening. This is still the Jewish rule for the Sabbath.

Jews today still keep strict rules on the Sabbath. In Israel, no buses run during the Sabbath, and of course the shops are closed. Many people do not use their cars on the Sabbath, or light a cooker. Some do not switch on the electric lights. They do not do any work themselves, or do anything which makes someone else work.

2 a What was the main purpose of the Sabbath?

   b When does the Sabbath begin?

   c Do you think that the idea of having a special day to think about God, and in which no one works, is a good one? Write down some reasons for your answer.

For discussion

3 Why do you think that the teachers of the Law were so shocked when Jesus claimed to forgive sins?

4 Read Mark 2:23–37. It was the Sabbath.

   a What did Jesus' disciples do wrong?

   b Write down why this was wrong.

   c Using verse 27, what did Jesus say about the Sabbath?

   d What do you think he might have meant by this?

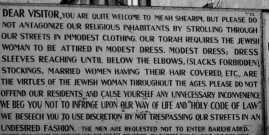

A Sign at Mea Shearim asking Gentiles to respect Jewish area

CONFLICT WITH THE AUTHORITIES

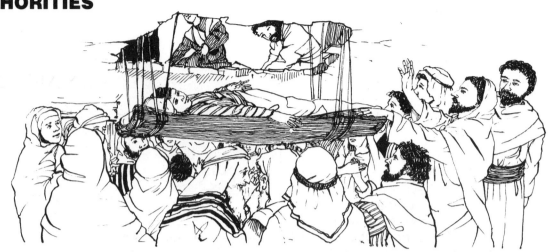

FURTHER ACTIVITIES

Jesus upsets people!

In Mark 2, Jesus upsets the Pharisees. They were the Jewish religious authorities, who tried to help the ordinary Jewish people to understand and obey the complex Jewish religious laws.

1 Read Mark 2:1–12.

In this section Jesus upsets the teachers of the law because he claims to forgive sins.

Copy and complete the chart. In column A you will find the name of a person or group of people. Write in column C what each of these says. The verse number in column B will help you.

A People	B Verse	C What each said
Jesus	5	
Teachers of the Law	7	
Jesus	9	
Jesus	10	
Jesus	11	
Everyone	12	

2 Read about Levi, or Matthew the tax collector, in Mark 2:13–17.

Look back at unit 3 to find out why the Jews hated tax collectors so much.

Write down, or record on tape, your own version of the conversations between A and B when Jesus had a meal at the tax collector's house.

Something to do

3 Read the letter from a teenage girl in Victorian England to her mother.

Imagine that you had built a time machine, and you returned to the year 1889. You have arrived on a Sunday, and discover that you are in church. Next, you return to a Victorian family's Sunday meal and spend the day as one of the family.

Describe what happened, and how Sunday in 1889 was different from a Sunday now.

The Old House
Willingworth
27th May 1889

Dearest Mamma,

Do come home soon from my aunt's house. We all miss you so much.

This last Sunday was spent going to the morning service at 11am. The servants went at 8am, but young Rose was ill so she remained at home. They got a good lunch for us. My youngest brother was very bored all Sunday. He said the Hymns were all about Death, and he objected to the starched collar and the ticklish material of his Sunday suit. I had to be strict with him to prevent him from playing with his top or any other of his toys. It was difficult too, to keep him from his books, or from walking in the woods. Neither did he wish to attend the afternoon service even though he was very bored. To entertain him on a Sunday, without doing the things of other days is a difficult task. Cook the ...ousehold matters. Cook

maid

SHOULD SUNDAY BE KEPT SPECIAL?

NAME (IN BLOCK CAPITALS   JOHN SMITH

AGE (tick correct box)   Under 11 ☐   11-15 ☑   16-18 ☐   18-21 ☐   22-30 ☐   30-45 ☐   Over 45 ☐

HOME ADDRESS (BLOCK CAPITALS) .12 STATION ROAD,...........
.CARDIFF...................................
....

POST CODE   ....

Do you work on Sundays   YES/NO

If YES, state type of work   ...Paper round...............

Are you a regular church goer?   YES/NO

Did you go to church last Sunday? YES/NO   Have you been to church in the last MONTH/YEAR? Yes

Tick which activities you normally enjoy on Sundays:

Visiting Friends	✓
Visiting relations	
Attending Sunday School/Youth Group/Church	Y.G.
Visiting places of interest	
Sport	✓
Homework	
Reading	
Staying in bed late — I'd like to!	✓
Listening to music	✓
Watching TV/Videos	✓
Playing Computer Games	
Looking after animals	
Other	

HOW DO YOU THINK JESUS WOULD WANT YOU TO SPEND SUNDAYS?

Do you think everyone should work on Sundays?   ...No........... Please return this questionnaire to:

Do you think all the shops should be open on Sundays?   Some shops......
R.E. DEPARTMENT
ROOM 36...........

Do you think Sundays should be a 'Special Day' different from all the others?   ..Yes...........

What is your favourite method of relaxing on Sundays?   .staying in bed..

Do you think Christians should go to church on Sundays?...............

Class activity

4 Design and carry out a survey to find out how people spend Sunday.

Your survey should include information about the age group of people being surveyed, as well as activities they might enjoy on Sundays.

You should include questions about whether they, or anyone in their family, attend church. The example above may help you. Discuss your findings in class.

Computer link

5 If you have access to a computer, you might like to design the form for your survey on it.

It would also be interesting to use a graphs program, if you have one, to display your results.

Many schools now are linked via electronic mail. If your school has a computer link like this, use the electronic mail to find another school to carry out your survey in a different area. It will be interesting to compare your results.

PRAYER IN A JEWISH HOME

Jesus grew up in a Jewish home, and like all other Jewish children, he would have learned the traditional Jewish prayers. Every morning and every evening, he would have been taught to say the **'Shema'**:

'Hear O Israel, the Lord your God is one Lord, and you shall love the Lord your God with all your heart, with all your soul, and with all your strength'.

A Scrolls of the Law

B The Sabbath meal

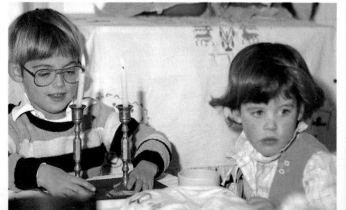

This is the central part of the Jewish faith. Christianity is also built on the idea of one God, who Christians worship by using the whole of their lives to serve him.

When Jesus had meals, the Bible tells us that he blessed and broke the bread. He would have said:

'Blessed art Thou, Lord God, King of the Universe, who brings forth bread from the ground'.

There were blessings for everything. Jews thanked God for everything they did.

JESUS TAUGHT HIS DISCIPLES TO PRAY

Jesus often went away on his own to pray. Sometimes, he would pray all night. He liked to go to very lonely places to pray.

One day, when he had gone away to pray, the disciples came to him and asked him to teach them to pray as well. They said that John the Baptist had taught his disciples a special prayer, and that they wanted Jesus to do the same. Jesus taught them the prayer which we now call the Lord's prayer:

C Jesus in the desert

'Father,
May your holy name be honoured,
May your kingdom come,
Give us day by day the food we need,
Forgive us our sins,
For we forgive everyone who does us wrong,
And do not bring us to any hard testing'.

(Luke 11:1–4)

ADVICE ABOUT PRAYER

Jesus went on to tell some stories which told his disciples more about prayer. He taught them to keep on asking, and their prayers would be answered. God, he said, was a loving Father, who knew how to give good things to all his children. If people ask God, then he will give them the Holy Spirit, which is the best gift anyone can have (Luke 11:5–9).

Jesus gave his followers some advice about praying. He said that it was wrong to make a great show of praying, and to pray in public places where everyone could see. He said that it was important to go somewhere quiet and undisturbed where people could pray to God in private. Prayers don't have to be long, he said. God doesn't answer prayers because they are long, but because he wants to give his children the things which they need (Matthew 6:5–7).

D Praying hands by Dürer

ANYONE CAN PRAY

In the **synagogues**, there always had to be at least ten men before they could pray together. Jesus said something very different. You don't need that number, he said. If any two or three of you agree together, and want to pray to God, he will hear you, and grant your requests. This was quite revolutionary. Jesus encouraged everyone to pray together, and to ask God to give them the things which they needed (Matthew 18:19–20).

E People praying at the Western wall

ACTIVITIES

1 a What does the 'Shema' tell Jews and Christians about what Jewish people believe about God?

   b Look at the 'Blessing for Bread'. Now write your own blessing for something you enjoy. It should begin:
   'Blessed art Thou, Lord God, King of the Universe . . .'

   c Why do you think Jesus went away on his own when he wanted to pray?

2 In Luke 11:5–9, there is a story which Jesus told about prayer. Read the story carefully.

   Either

   a Write a poem which tells this story.

   Or

   b In a group, work out how you could act this story. It could make a very amusing play . . . don't worry, Jesus wanted people to laugh when he told the story in the first place!

Don't be weary in prayer

3 Look at Matthew 6:5–7.

   a Why do you think that Jesus calls the people who make a public show of praying where everyone is sure to see them, 'hypocrites'?

   b Using verse 6 to help you, write down some advice which you think Jesus might have given to a young person who wanted to pray to God.

   c Why do you think Jesus tells people not to use a lot of meaningless words when they pray?

   d Do you think Jesus would prefer people to pray in their own words or to read prayers from a book? Write down some reasons for your answer.

FURTHER ACTIVITIES

Muslims pray by bowing down and facing Mecca.

Jews prayed with their hands in the air in the time of Jesus.

Now, Jews like to pray near the Western Wall – the only bit left of the Old Temple.

Many Christians kneel to pray (especially in church).

Some Christians use beads called a rosary to help them pray.

Some people pray on the bus!

The Bible says 'Pray at all times'.

Some people pray in bed!

God doesn't really mind too much how you stand, sit, or even jump for joy. He just wants you to keep in touch!

Some people pray in the bath!

1 Why do you think Jesus told people to pray?

JESUS TEACHING ABOUT PRAYER

2 Read Matthew 6:5–14. Jesus taught his followers how they should pray.

a Use verses 9–13 to copy this version of the Lord's Prayer into your books.

b In Luke 11:1–4, you will find another version of the same prayer.

3 Copy and complete the following chart, using the three different versions of the Lord's Prayer.

Church	Matthew 6:9–13	Luke 11:1–4
a Our Father in Heaven		
b Hallowed be your name		
c Your kingdom come		
d Your will be done on earth as it is in heaven		
e Give us today our daily bread		
f Forgive us our sins		
g As we forgive those who sin against us		
h Lead us not into temptation		
i But deliver us from evil		
j For the Kingdom, the power, and the glory are yours, now and for ever.		

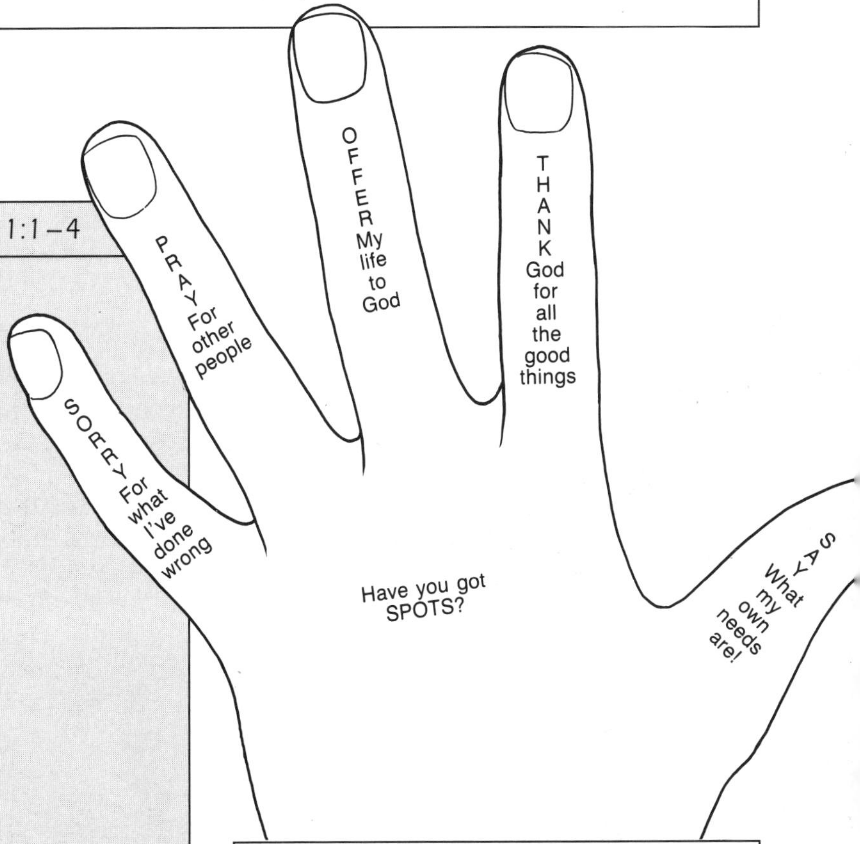

4 Give us this day our daily bread.

a Why do you think that Jesus says **our** daily bread, not **my** daily bread?

b Do you think that when people say this prayer, it should make them try to help people who do not have enough to eat?

Write down some reasons for your answer.

c Make a list of some of the ways in which Christians (and others) could make sure that everyone does have 'daily bread'.

PRAY For other people

OFFER My life to God

THANK God for all the good things

SORRY For what I've done wrong

Have you got SPOTS?

SAYS What my own needs are!

PRAYER SPOTS

5 Draw around your own hand, and then copy the things which are written in each finger.

These are some of the things which Christians (and Jews, and others) do when they pray.

Think of the kind of things you would say, as you get to each finger.

Can you spot the reasons why Christians include these things in their prayers?

While Jesus was wandering around Israel preaching and teaching, he met lots of different people. Some of them wanted to follow him. Some wanted to find out more about him. Here are some stories about some of the people Jesus met.

NICODEMUS

Nicodemus was a **Pharisee**, and one of the Jewish leaders. He wanted to find out more about Jesus, but was possibly afraid of what his friends might say. So he went to see Jesus at night.

He was already sure that Jesus was sent by God. He said that no one could do the **miracles** which Jesus did unless God was with him.

Jesus told Nicodemus that anyone who wanted to be part of the Kingdom of God needed to be 'born again'. The Pharisee did not understand this. Jesus was saying that people needed to allow God to rule their lives. This was like a completely new start in life, so Jesus called it being 'born again'.

ZACCHAEUS

When Jesus was passing through Jericho, on his way to Jerusalem, he met a **tax collector**. His name was Zacchaeus, and he was very rich.

Zacchaeus was a very small man. He had to climb a sycamore tree so that he could see Jesus. He may not have wanted to be noticed looking out for Jesus, as he was a rich tax collector who was despised by the Jews.

When Jesus came near to him, he looked up into the tree and saw Zacchaeus. 'Come on down, Zacchaeus', he said, I'd like to stay in your house today'. Usually, a **Rabbi**, or religious person, would not go near the house of a tax collector, because they worked for the Romans, and were often thought to be dishonest. So Zacchaeus was delighted at the idea of Jesus coming to his home.

The people who were watching weren't so happy, though! They thought it was wrong of Jesus to go and eat with a man they thought was a sinner.

Zacchaeus stopped cheating people that day. He promised to pay back four times as much as he had overcharged to anyone that he had cheated. He also promised to give half of his possessions to the poor. Jesus was thrilled that the man had made this decision. To find out what Jesus said, read the whole story in Luke 19:1–9.

THE RICH YOUNG MAN

Sometimes people say Jesus was mainly interested in poor people. In fact, he was interested in everyone, both rich and poor.

One day, a rich young man came to see Jesus. He very much wanted to serve God, and asked Jesus for help. Jesus told him to keep the Ten Commandments. 'I've done all that', the young man said, 'In fact, I've been doing it all my life! What else do you think I ought to do?' Jesus told the young man to sell everything that he had, and give the money to the poor, and then come with him.

Pharisees helped ordinary people understand the Law

WELCOME TO JERICHO

The young man was very rich. This was more than he could manage to do. He went away miserable. Jesus was upset about it too. He had liked the young man as soon as he saw him. He said that it was very hard for rich people to let their lives be ruled by God. In fact, he said, it was harder to get a rich man into heaven, than it was to thread a needle with a camel!

Peter pointed out that he and the other disciples had left everything to follow Jesus. He had been willing to give up his trade of fishing to come with Jesus. Jesus promised the disciples that they would not regret it.

Sadducees were usually priests and they were often rich!

NOTES/DATABASE

Use the glossary to look up the meanings of the following words. Then use the definitions to make your own notes or suitable entries on your database.

Pharisee   Rabbi

Miracle   Sadducee

Tax Collector

NICODEMUS

1 Read John 3:1–12.

a Why do you think that Nicodemus went to visit Jesus at night?

b Use verse 2 to help you to write down the reason why Nicodemus and the Pharisees knew that Jesus had come from God.

c What did Jesus say had to happen for someone to 'see the Kingdom of God'?

d What do you think Jesus meant when he said that Nicodemus needed to be 'born again'?

ACTIVITIES

ZACCHAEUS

2 Read Luke 19:1–9.

a Why was Zacchaeus' job disliked so much by the Jews?

b Why do you think that Zacchaeus climbed the sycamore tree?

c How did Jesus react when he saw Zacchaeus in the tree?

d How did Zacchaeus change his lifestyle after he had met Jesus?

THE RICH YOUNG MAN

3 Read Matthew 19:16–24.

a What was the first question that the young man asked?

b How did Jesus answer him?

c When the young man said that he had kept all those commandments all his life, but wanted to do something more, what did Jesus suggest?

d Why do you think that the young man did not do as Jesus suggested?

For discussion

4 The rich young man was told to sell all his possessions and to give all the money to the poor.

Discuss whether you think all Christians should do this.

SOME PEOPLE JESUS MET

FURTHER ACTIVITIES

JESUS MEETS A WOMAN FROM SAMARIA

1 Draw your own sandglass and fill in all the times correctly.

Did you know?

People used sandglasses to tell the time before they invented clocks.

Map work

2 Look at the map.

This shows you the route which Jesus and his disciples took when they walked from Capernaum to Jerusalem. Now answer these questions.

a What was the country like?

b Why do you think they stopped at Jacob's Well?

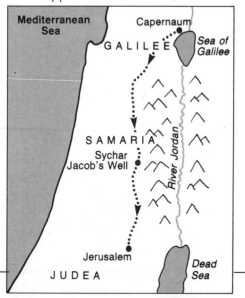

British Standard Time (BST)	New Testament Time
6 p.m.	12th hour
5 p.m.	11th hour
4 p.m.	10th hour
3 p.m.	9th hour
2 p.m.	8th hour
1 p.m.	7th hour
12 a.m.	6th hour
11 a.m.	5th hour
10 a.m.	4th hour
9 a.m.	3rd hour
8 a.m.	2nd hour
7 a.m.	1st hour

TIME

12 a.m.	6th hour

B.S.T.	BIBLE

3 Read John 4:1–26.

a What time was it?

b What reasons can you think of for the woman choosing the hottest part of the day to go to the well?

c Why was she surprised when Jesus spoke to her? (Verse 9)

d Look carefully at verses 20–21.

i Where did the Jews worship?

ii Where did the Samaritans worship?

iii Read verse 23. What does Jesus say about true worship?

iv Read verses 25–26. What did Jesus tell the woman about himself?

SOME PEOPLE JESUS MET

Dear Mum,
   Just a line from Jericho to tell you that we are on our way to Jerusalem. Crowds to meet us here in Jericho. One bloke wanted to see Jesus so much he climbed into a tree! He was a tax collector – and Jesus picked his house to stay at. Fabulous meal – he could afford it. Anyway, this chap decided to give back all the money he'd cheated people out of. Jesus was thrilled.
   Love
   Peter.

Mrs bar Jonah,

1, Fisherman's Terrace,

Capernaum,

Galilee.

A Jericho, ancient ruins

4 Imagine you are James or John. Send your own postcard home to your family in Capernaum. Design a picture for the front of the postcard as well as writing a message on the back. The message should describe what has been happening in Jericho.

Invitation

Simon the Pharisee requests the pleasure of the company of... *Jesus of Nazareth*...for dinner on Wednesday evening at 8 p.m.

Prayer shawls will be worn.   R.S.V.P.

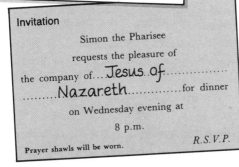

"I've got that fellow what's his name...er...Jesus of Nazareth coming to dinner tomorrow. You must come...Oh good...Well, why don't you come about 7.30p.m.? I've invited him for eight. It'll give us time to get our feet washed before he arrives...Gosh, no! not _His_ feet! He won't expect _that_!"

Home sweet ☀home☀

5 Luke 7:36–50 tells the story of the dinner party.
   Draw your own series of pictures, or write an account of what happened at the dinner party, including the arrival of an unexpected guest!

It was considered polite to wash guests' feet when they arrived at your house. Now read on.

WHO IS REALLY IMPORTANT?

6 a Place the following people in the order you would think important:

doctor   child   housewife
tramp   clown   Prime Minister
teacher   cook

b Now rewrite the list, putting yourself in at the place where you think you should be.
   You might think that you were the most important, or the least important, or somewhere in the middle!

c Read the story of Simon's dinner party again. Now think about the way Jesus treated people.

Discuss: Which order do you think Jesus would have put people in? Give some reasons for the way you answer this.

Jesus used his **miracles** and his preaching to show his **disciples** who he actually was. At the beginning of his **ministry**, he read from the Isaiah scroll in the synagogue. He read the part where it said that the Messiah would make blind people see, deaf people hear, and lame people walk, and poor people would hear the 'Good News' (Luke 4:16–20).

When John the Baptist's disciples asked Jesus if he was the Messiah, he didn't say yes or no, but instead pointed to what was happening (Luke 7:18–23).

So, the disciples had the evidence. Jesus had not actually said that he was the Messiah. He wanted people to work it out for themselves. Jesus knew that people were talking about him. But what were they saying about him? Had anyone reached the right conclusion?

WHO AM I?

Jesus asked the disciples a question. 'Who does everybody say that I am?' 'Well', they replied. 'There are some people who are saying you are Elijah.' 'Yes, and some others who reckon you're one of the **prophets**!' 'Some of them even reckon you're John the Baptist, come back from the dead.'

There were lots of suggestions about who Jesus might be. You can imagine the chatter and laughter that accompanied a conversation like this! Then Jesus came to the real point of the question. 'What about you? Who do you say that I am?'

Maybe the laughter ceased, and they fell silent. The atmosphere might have changed from one of fun to one of great seriousness as Jesus asked this question.

Finally, Simon Peter spoke up. 'You are the Christ, the Son of the Living God'. At this point, the atmosphere must have been electric, as they all realized that Peter was right. No one had dared to say it before. Each time someone had called out in the street that he was the Messiah, Jesus had quickly silenced that

person. They must have been nervous about Jesus' possible reaction.

YOU ARE THE CHRIST

This time it was different. Jesus had asked the question. He wanted to know whether the disciples had in fact worked it out for themselves, and this was the reply he wanted. Jesus was pleased with Simon. He said that Simon wasn't saying it just because that was what other people were saying, but because God had revealed it to him.

This was the moment when Simon bar John got his new name. Jesus nicknamed him Peter, because this means 'rock'.

At first
Jesus said to Simon (Peter)

Soon
Peter became Bishop of Rome

Later
Other men became Bishop of Rome – one after the other.
The Roman Catholic Church, the largest group of Christians, believes all these Bishops inherited Peter's right to be leader.

People loved the Bishop of Rome so much they called him 'Papa', or 'Dad'. This is how we get the word 'Pope'.

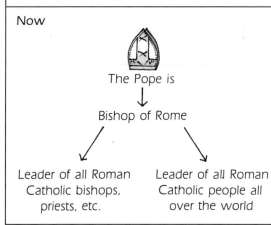

Now

The Pope is
↓
Bishop of Rome
↓   ↓
Leader of all Roman Catholic bishops, priests, etc.   Leader of all Roman Catholic people all over the world

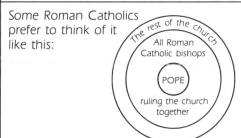

Some Roman Catholics prefer to think of it like this:

The rest of the church
All Roman Catholic bishops
POPE
ruling the church together

All Roman Catholic bishops lead and guide the church together but the Pope is the senior bishop who speaks for all of them together

Jesus said Simon Peter's faith was the rock, or foundation, on which the church was to be built. It was so firm a foundation that nothing would ever overcome it.

Read Matthew 16:13–20.

Later on, Peter became a leader of the church, first of all in Jerusalem, and later on in Rome. He was probably the first Bishop of Rome. He was crucified in Rome during the reign of the Emperor Nero.

THE PROTESTANT VIEW

The Protestant churches (Christians who are not Roman Catholics) do not accept the leadership of the Bishop of Rome in this way. They believe that when Jesus said, 'On this rock I will build my Church', he was referring to Peter's faith. It was faith that was to be the foundation on which the church was to be built.

NOTES/DATABASE

Use the glossary to look up the meanings of the following words. Then use the definitions to make your own notes or suitable entries on your database.

Miracle	Prophet
Disciple	Pope
Ministry	

ACTIVITIES

1 a Which ways did Jesus use to show the disciples who he really was?

b What kind of things did Isaiah expect the disciples to do?

c Look at Luke 7:18–23 to find out how Jesus answered the disciples of John the Baptist when they asked him whether or not he was the Messiah. Write down what you have found out.

d What evidence do you think that the disciples already had, to help them understand who Jesus really was?

Drama

4 In groups plan a short play which tells the story of what happened in Matthew 16:13–20.

Use the information in this unit to help you do this.

What did Simon say to Jesus?

What did Jesus say to Simon?

2 Draw the pictures. Use Matthew 16:16–20 to fill in the speech bubbles correctly.

Clue:

granite!

For discussion

3 Peter had worked out that Jesus was the Messiah. Many Jews believed that the Messiah would lead an army to fight the Romans. Some Jews thought that when the Messiah came there would be a thousand years of peace when the Jews would be the most important nation.

What do you think that the disciples expected Jesus to do, now that they knew he was the Messiah?

A A possible site where Jesus said 'You are Peter'

FURTHER ACTIVITIES

SOME SPECIAL NAMES FOR JESUS

A The Christ or the Messiah

Christ and Messiah have exactly the same meaning.

Christ is a Greek word meaning 'the anointed one', and Messiah is a Hebrew word also meaning 'the anointed one'.

Kings were anointed (had oil poured over them) at their coronation. This gave them the special authority to be king.

For a long time, the Jews had expected a Messiah to come and teach them about God. Some Jews expected him to be a great fighter who would drive the Romans out.

1 Look up the references in the chart, and fill in what it tells you about the Messiah.

B The Son of Man

Jesus often called himself the Son of Man. There are two occasions in the Old Testament when this title is used.

a Daniel 7:13 – where the Son of Man is given royal power.

b Psalm 8:4 – where it means ordinary man.

In the time of Jesus, people were known as 'Son of . . .' and their father's name. If you translate 'Son of Man' into Hebrew (the language of the Jews) it becomes 'ben Adam'. Christians, Jews and Muslims believe Adam was the name of the first man. It is also an ordinary Hebrew word meaning 'man'. By using the name 'Son of Man', Jesus was claiming royal power (Daniel 7) and saying that he was a representative of all men (Psalm 8:4).

C Lamb of God

When he saw Jesus, John the Baptist said 'Here is the lamb of God who takes away the sin of the world'. On the night before the Israelites (old word for Jews) left Egypt, they were told to kill a lamb and to put some of its blood on the doorposts of their houses. (Read the story in Exodus 12:21–28.) Each year after that, the Israelites celebrated a festival called Passover. This remembers the time when the Israelites left Egypt.

Jesus is called the Lamb of God, because Christians believe he died to lead the people into a new relationship with God. Eating the Passover lamb had been the first step on the way out of Egypt and into the Promised Land for the Jews. So Jesus is thought of as being a way to God in the same way as the Passover lamb was the beginning of the way to the Promised Land.

Bible references	What it tells you about the Messiah
Isaiah 11:1–9	
Isaiah 9:6f	

2 Draw these think bubbles with the words inside.

Look up the Bible references in the table below, and match the correct reference with the think bubble. Then write under each think bubble the name of the person who said each of these things.

Bible reference	Person
John 1:29	John the Baptist
Matthew 16:16	Simon Peter
Mark 2:28	Jesus

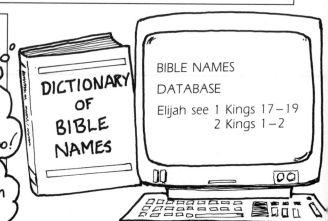

Look, here comes the Lamb of God who takes away the sins of the world

The Son of Man is in charge of the Sabbath too!

You are the Christ, the Son of the Living God

DICTIONARY OF BIBLE NAMES

BIBLE NAMES DATABASE
Elijah see 1 Kings 17–19
2 Kings 1–2

Life giver/You are the Christ
by Jimmy and Carol Owens

Who is this who has life to give?
Who is this who tells the dead to live?
Not an ordinary man with some words
    of truth to say,
Has his moments in the sun and one
    day fades away!

Who is this who has life to give?
Who is this who tells the dead to live?
Not an ordinary man but one who
    dares to say
That He is the Resurrection and the life
And then offers it to you and me.

Come to the Life Giver!
Come to the Life Giver
And let Him pour His life on you!
Let Him pour His life on you!
Let Him pour His life on you!

Come to the Life Giver!
Jesus the Life Giver!
And let Him pour His life on you!
Let Him pour His life on you!
Let Him pour His life on you!

Who am I? What are they saying?
Do they know the truth or are they
    blind?
Who am I? What do you call Me?
Tell Me, what is My name?

You are the Christ.
The Son of the Living God!
I say You are the Christ,
The Son of the Living God!
You are the Christ!
You are the Lord!

You are the Christ,
The Son of the Living God!
I say You are the Christ,
The Son of the Living God!
You are the Christ!
You are my Lord!

For discussion

3 In a small group, discuss why you think Jesus is called the 'Life Giver' in this song.

B The Vatican

4 Look up **Elijah** and **John the Baptist** in a dictionary of Bible names, and add each of them to your database or notes.

SUCCESSOR TO PETER?

5 Use the information in this unit to help you to answer these questions.

a How do Roman Catholic Christians believe that the **Pope** receives the right to be the leader of all the Roman Catholics in the world?

b Write down the reason why the Bishop of Rome was called the Pope.

6 Draw a chart like the one below. In column A write down the Catholic viewpoint about the Pope. In column B write down what some Catholics believe about the Pope. In column C write down what Protestant Christians believe that Jesus meant when he said, 'On this rock I will build my Church'.

A Catholic view	B What some Catholics believe	C What Protestants believe Jesus meant

Group work

7 a Find some newspaper cuttings about the Pope, and the kind of things which he does now. You will probably find new reports from the countries he visits.
    Make a book of information about the Pope.

b Jesus' disciples went all over the world telling people about Jesus, and encouraging Christians wherever they met them. They became known as Apostles. This means people who have been sent out with a special message.

Look up Peter and Paul in a Bible dictionary or Bible names database. Find out about the kind of things which Peter and Paul did.
    Now discuss the similarities which you can find between the things which Peter and Paul did, and the kind of things which the Pope does now.

Peter said that Jesus was really the **Messiah**, or Christ, and the Son of the Living God. That seems to have been a turning point in the life of Jesus. After that he allowed people to say that he was the Christ, instead of forbidding them to tell anyone. He also began to tell the disciples that he was soon going to be put to death and would come alive again three days later.

THE TRANSFIGURATION

(Mark 9:2–13, Luke 9:28–36, Matthew 17:1–13.)

Jesus took his special friends Peter, James and John, and they climbed up a mountain together. Luke's Gospel says it was so that they could pray in a quiet place.

When they got to the top of the mountain, Jesus began to pray. His disciples watched him, and as he prayed, his clothes became dazzling white. This event became known as the **Transfiguration**. Mark's Gospel adds a lovely touch to the story (Mark 9:2f).

Next, the disciples saw that Jesus was talking to Moses and Elijah. In the Bible, Moses always represents the Law (first

five books of the Bible) and Elijah always represents the **prophets**.

When the disciples saw Jesus with these two very important people, they realized once again that Jesus must be a very important religious leader. Peter then suggested that they should make some shelters for the three of them. What Peter probably had in mind was the festival of **Sukkot**, when the Jewish people make shelters from branches. They live and pray in these shelters to thank God for leading them out of Egypt into the **Promised Land** of Israel.

After Peter had made this suggestion, a cloud appeared, and they all felt its shadow over them. In the Old Testament, a cloud is the symbol of God being present. Read Mark 1:11, and see how God spoke to Jesus when he was baptized. In the same way, God spoke

C Sukkot

about Jesus now. The voice said, 'This is my own dear son, listen to Him'.

The disciples were frightened. This event was, after all, such a strange happening. They had never before experienced anything like it. However, after seeing the cloud and hearing the voice of God, the disciples could have had no further doubts about whether or not Jesus was the Messiah.

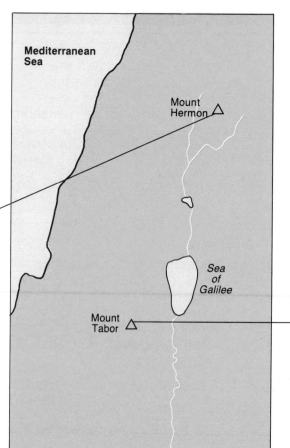

Mediterranean Sea

Mount Hermon △

Sea of Galilee

Mount Tabor △

A Mount Hermon

Two possible sites for the Transfiguration are Mount Tabor or Mount Hermon.

B Mount Tabor

RISING FROM THE DEAD

On the way down the mountain, Jesus told the disciples not to tell anyone what they had seen until after he had risen from the dead. They didn't know what rising from the dead meant, so they asked Jesus.

The disciples asked why the teachers of religion (the **Pharisees** and the **scribes**) suggested that Elijah had to come again before the Messiah came. Jesus told them that Elijah had already come again, and was treated very badly by the Jews. He was telling them that John the Baptist was in fact Elijah. By now, the disciples were sure that Jesus was the Messiah. It was time to head for Jerusalem.

NOTES/DATABASE

Use the glossary to look up the meanings of the following words. Then use the definitions to make your own notes or suitable entries on your database.

Messiah	Promised Land
Transfiguration	Pharisees
Prophets	Scribes
Sukkot	

ACTIVITIES

1 Read Mark 9:2–8 very carefully.

  a Draw a picture of the scene on the top of the mountain as you think it might have looked.

  b Who did Jesus take with him?

  c Why do you think he chose these particular people?

2 Peter was a very impetuous man. Sometimes he said the very first thing which came into his head, without really thinking about it.

  a Write down what Peter said on this occasion. How did Jesus react? Why do you think that Jesus reacted like this?

  b What reason might Peter have had for making the suggestion that they build these little 'booths'?

3 Draw the pictures below and fill in the speech bubbles correctly.

  a Mark 1 (see unit 2)

  b Mark 9 (see this unit)

  c The voice which Jesus heard when he was baptized came at a turning point in his life. Do you think this voice from heaven also marks a turning point in Jesus' life? If so, what do you think that turning point might be?

c Use a Bible encyclopaedia to help you find out more about the Jewish festival of Sukkot. A Jewish friend might be able to tell you more about the way in which the festival is celebrated now.

  Write down what you can learn about Sukkot from the pictures.

4 Imagine you are Peter.

Use the information in this unit and in Mark 9:2–8 to write about the day when you climbed a mountain with Jesus and some other friends.

FURTHER ACTIVITIES

1 a What were the names of the people who were seen talking with Jesus?

  b Use Exodus 19 and I Kings 19 to help you to find out what happened when these people met with God on the top of a mountain. Write a short talk to explain to the rest of the class who these people were.

  c Discuss the reasons why you think Moses and Elijah were with Jesus.
    Use the pictures on this page to help you as well as looking up Moses and Elijah on your Bible database or in your Bible dictionary.

Who was Moses?

READ ALL ABOUT IT

MOSES
—Exodus 1-end

ELIJAH
1 Kings 17-19.

Moses represents the Law.

1-5 The Commandments

6-10 The Commandments

Mount Sinai where Moses met God and was given the law.

Who was Elijah?

The Presence of God

"This is what God says"

Elijah represents the prophets.

Mount Horeb where Elijah met God — who showed him that he was present in a "still small voice."

A LETTER FROM ISRAEL

2 Look at the postcard from Mount Tabor which shows the inside and outside of the Church of the Transfiguration.

Read through the letter. Use these resources to help you write your own letter describing a day's outing to Mount Tabor. You might like to imagine you walked up as well as down!

Shalom from Mount Tabor

3 Now read Mark 9:14–29.

When Jesus and his friends arrived at the bottom of the mountain, they were greeted by this . . .

Lawyers

Dad and boy

Disciples

Argument

So Jesus said . . .

'What's all this about?'

. . . so they told him!

Complete the story by drawing **three** more cartoons to show what happened next.

Kibbutz Degania,
Galilee,
Israel.

Shalom,

(Thats how they begin letters and answer the phone here in Israel). Thought you'd like to know how the trip to Israel is going. We are staying in the Kibbutz Degania in Galilee. This is a kind of community where families all live together in one place. Mums and Dads have separate rooms, but children all live with their own age groups.

Today we drove to Mount Tabor. It was so steep I thought the car was going to fall off the road - and there was no fence on the edge of the road!

Mount Tabor is the place they think that Jesus was "transfigured." It certainly looks likely. When we got to the top, there was a fantastic view - all across Galilee. We could see for miles! There was a church at the top. I thought that was rather weird because Jesus told Peter not to build a shrine there! It's a very beautiful church, but I wondered what Jesus would have thought of it.

We decided to walk down the Mountain. Jesus and His disciples walked both ways. It must have taken them all day. We were exhausted when we got back to Degania.

By the way, did you know that the Sea of Galilee is 600ft below sea level, and that it is the only place in the world where Peterfish are found. They are delicious.

4 Using verses 17 and 18, make a list of what was wrong with the boy.

Today we know about a disease called epilepsy. The boy in this story might have had epilepsy. Find out as much as you can about epilepsy. You might like to write to The Epileptic Society.

5 Read verses 23 and 24.

Draw speech bubbles to say what Jesus said, and what the boy's father said.

ON THE ROAD

Jesus was now ready to begin on his final journey to Jerusalem. He had prepared his disciples as well as he could for his death and rising again. The disciples had not liked Jesus telling them that he was going to die. In fact, they proved that they did not really understand by arguing about which one of them would be the greatest in the Kingdom of Heaven (Mark 9:33–37). To settle the argument, Jesus put a little child in the middle of them. 'If you want to be great then you've got to be like this child.' Look at verse 35 to find out what Jesus thought about being a real leader.

The road to Jerusalem from Galilee was long and hard. Jesus went along the Jordan valley to Jericho, and then up through the desert to Jerusalem.

Some of the people he met on the journey wanted to come with him. There was the rich young man (Mark 10:17–25) who cared too much about his many possessions to really follow Jesus. Then there was the man who said he would follow Jesus wherever he went (Luke 9:57).

To those who would have liked to have followed Jesus, he said that anyone who wanted to be his follower must be single minded about it. 'No one, who starts ploughing, and then looks back, is fit for the Kingdom of God' (Luke 9:62).

A On the way to Jerusalem

THE HEALING OF A BLIND MAN

Some people were healed as Jesus travelled to Jerusalem. Mark 10:46–52 tells us about a blind man who recovered his sight. He was regarded by everyone as of so little importance, he didn't even have a name of his own. He was known as 'Bartimaeus', or 'Son of Timaeus'. He sat by the roadside on the way to Jericho and called out, 'Son of David, have mercy on me'. By calling Jesus 'Son of David', he was calling him the Messiah. On this occasion Jesus did not tell him to be quiet, as he had done to others who called out in a similar way. Instead, Jesus stopped, and called the man to him. Struggling to his feet, Bartimaeus blindly made his way to Jesus. Seconds later his desire to see was granted (Mark 10:46–52).

Lazarus come out!

Bethany, where Jesus brought Lazarus back to life again.

LAZARUS IS RAISED FROM THE DEAD

Before he reached Jerusalem, Jesus received news that his close friend Lazarus was dead. It was several days before Jesus came to Bethany, where Lazarus lived. When he arrived, Lazarus was already dead. He had been wrapped in tight burial clothes, and put into a rock tomb four days earlier. Lazarus' sisters believed that if Jesus had been there, Lazarus would still have been alive. They believed that God would answer any prayer which Jesus made (John 11:22). When Jesus was taken to the tomb, he asked to have the heavy stone which guarded the entrance removed. Then he prayed (John 11:41f) and called to Lazarus to come out. Still wrapped in the grave clothes, Lazarus came out of the tomb.

Did you know?

There is enough salt in the Mount of Sodom to keep the earth supplied for the next 250 thousand years.

In Jericho, Jesus met Zacchaeus, a tax collector who climbed a tree, and he also healed a blind man.

GALILEE

As they went along, the disciples argued about who would be the greatest.

River Jordan

Phew!

Did you know?

The highest temperature ever recorded on earth was near Jericho, on the shores of the Dead Sea.

B Nurse giving a child treatment in Jerusalem

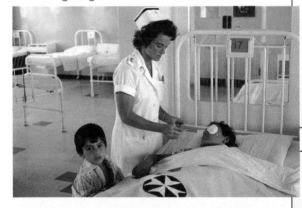

C Blind person working at printing press

ACTIVITIES

1 Draw a map to show the route which Jesus took along the Jordan valley from Galilee to Jerusalem.

   Mark the route clearly. (Use the map in unit 1 to help you.)

2 Either

   a Imagine you were one of the disciples travelling with Jesus to Jerusalem. Describe carefully the events that took place on one particular day, and include how you would feel about the long, hard trek.

      Or

   b Read Luke 9:57–62.

      Imagine that you were one of the people who wanted to follow Jesus. Describe how you might have felt when you heard his reply, and describe what you might have done next.

'THE BLIND SEE'
LUKE 7:22. ISAIAH 35:5A

Drama

Split into groups of 8–10.
   Read Mark 10:46–52, which is about Bartimaeus. Decide how you are going to act this story. Try to make sure you have the right people for each part. Don't forget the stage-hands are important too.

D Guide dog

One of the things which the Messiah was expected to do was to heal blind people. In Luke 7:22 Jesus himself pointed to that as proof that he was the Messiah. Healing Bartimaeus on the way to Jerusalem was another way in which Jesus was showing he was the Messiah.

THE TORCH HOUSE TRUST

The Torch House Trust does not heal blind people, but it does help them to find out about Jesus – by publishing Bibles and Christian books in Braille, as well as talking books, i.e. audio-tapes which have the whole book on them, often read by the author.

3 a Look at the three pictures on this page of ways of helping blind people. Explain how each of them in different ways is continuing the work Jesus began.

   b Find out about a rather special lady called **Helen Keller**. Then write a short booklet about her which could be used by younger children.

   c See if you can find someone to show you some Braille – you will find it fascinating. Why would Braille be useful to a blind person?

   d In what ways do you think your life would be different if you were blind?

JOURNEY TO JERUSALEM

FURTHER ACTIVITIES

Leader	The qualities you would look for
1 Captain of a football/netball team	
2 Form prefect	
3 Conductor of an orchestra	
4 Swimming captain	
5 Captain of an athletics team	
6 Organizer of a litter collection at school	

1 What do you feel are the qualities of a good leader?

a To find out, first of all, complete the chart.

b Do you always choose the person who is best at that activity? Give some reasons for your answer.

c Make a list of the qualities you think are most important in a leader.

d Use Mark 9:33–37 and Mark 10:35–45 to help you answer this question.

Write down the qualities which you think Jesus thought were important in a leader.

2 Read the passage called Bethany.

Now answer the following questions.

a Where was Mrs Windsor going when she set out from Jerusalem?

b What did the sign by the roadside tell them about?

c What was special about the two storeyed building?

d How do we know that the owner of the building was probably an olive oil dealer?

e Using your dictionary, find out what 'venerated' means.

f When they followed the path over rocky ground what did they find?

g What is an archaeologist?

h What did the archaeologists think happened at this place?

i Why do you think the travellers found this place so exciting?

BETHANY

We had set out from Jerusalem in the direction of Jericho. It was not long before we reached the tiny village of Bethany. Clinging to the barren hillside we might have driven through it without even noticing. A sign on the roadside led us to investigate the church which was dedicated to St. Lazarus. I can't remember much about the church, except that it was small, and typical of so many churches in the Middle east. We left the church by a different door, and found ourselves in the courtyard of a Roman house. Through the courtyard was another gate which led us to the bottom of a two storied building hewn from the rock. In the middle stood an Olive Press, apparently one of two which had served Jerusalem at the time of Jesus. The owner of the house must have been an olive oil dealer. Further surprises were in store for us as we climbed the stone stairway to the living-quarters upstairs. These had signs of having been venerated, as early as the second century, as a Christian shrine. Leaving by a tiny doorway, we followed the path across rocky ground, until we came to a rock hewn tomb. This, a sign told us was believed to be the tomb from which Lazarus was raised from the dead. Archaeologists in the 1960's had discovered this place, and the evidence they found showed that it had been venerated as the place where Jesus raised Lazarus from the dead since the second century. It had disappeared from sight, and was not discovered until the wave of archaeology which followed the Six Days War. It was exciting to find this particular place. It had not been in any of the guide books, and we felt as though we had discovered it ourselves.

G. Windsor.

E Lazarus lived here

Drama

3 a It would be fun to write a short play about Lazarus. Don't forget to include sadness, fear and amazement in your play. Then you can act out the various parts you have written. Ask your teacher first, but perhaps you could make your desks form the tomb.

b In a group of about six, imagine you are the production team for Radio Jerusalem. You will need to interview eye-witnesses and to present an in-depth report from Bethany, the scene of this event. Try to imagine what the religious authorities might have thought. (Use John 11:45–53 to help you.) You might include an interview with Caiaphas. You could record your news report on tape.

4 Read the newspaper article.

Now write a letter to the Editor. The address is circled on the newspaper.

JERUSALEM THIS WEEK

'LAZARUS COME OUT'

Almost 800 years ago, the prophet Isaiah told us that when the Messiah comes he will raise the dead. Over the last three years we have watched with interest as Jesus of Nazareth has fulfilled each of the prophecies made about the Messiah. We have seen the blind see and the lame walk. Most miraculous of all, we have seen Jesus telling the Good News about God to the poor. Now it seems, he has found a way of convincing some people that he can also raise the dead.

The man concerned is a close friend of Jesus. It seems that he was ill, and sent for Jesus expecting Jesus to come and heal him.

Jesus was apparently informed of the illness, but, we are told, delayed before coming south to his friend. We are told that Jesus was very upset when he heard that Lazarus, a wealthy olive merchant, was dead. Jesus was taken by Lazarus' two sisters, Martha and Mary, to the rock tomb as soon as he arrived. After praying, he called 'Lazarus come out'. At once Lazarus appeared.

It would seem likely that this was a hoax, concocted by the two friends to add weight to the claim that Jesus is the Messiah. It does, however, seem unlikely that so many people, who all saw it happen, could be fooled. There are many witnesses prepared to swear that Lazarus had been dead and buried for four days before Jesus arrived. Many of the witnesses may well have been confused. It could be that they all looked away at the moment when Lazarus emerged and so failed to see what really happened.

Caiaphas and the religious leaders are reported to be looking for a reason to arrest Jesus before he can begin to turn the world upside down.

Moses bar None, Jerusalem

LAZARUS RAISED

Amateur photographer Aaron Ishead was right on target for another brilliant picture yesterday. Pictured on the left is the scene, snapped by him in Bethany. Jesus of Nazareth, so they say, visited the tomb of a friend, and ended up raising him from the dead.

Is this a hoax? Could it be a conjuring trick by the clever young rabbi? Could so many people have been fooled?

Any readers letters on this subject will be printed. They should be addressed to:
'The Editor', *Jerusalem Times*, Religious Education Department.

F 'Lazarus come out'

A Jerusalem from the Mount of Olives

B Working donkey outside Lion's Gate

> **Zechariah 9:9 and 14:4**
>
> **Rejoice greatly, O daughter of Zion, for behold, your King comes to you, riding on a donkey.**
>
> **The Lord will come . . . His feet will be upon the Mount of Olives.**

THE PASSION

One of the first parts of the life of Jesus to be written down was the events of the last week of his life. This is called the **Passion Narrative**. It begins when Jesus rode into Jerusalem on a donkey. Christians call the day when he did this Palm Sunday.

This part was written down first because it was important for Christians to know about the death and **Resurrection** of Jesus.

FULFILLING PROPHECIES

Read Mark 11:1–11.

When Jesus rode into Jerusalem on the back of a donkey, it was like saying to the world, 'Look, here I am, I'm the Messiah'. Jesus was telling everyone, by his actions, that he was the Messiah they had all been waiting for. Look in the boxes on this page to see which Old Testament prophecy Jesus was fulfilling this time.

Very often, in the Old Testament, prophets acted out what they wanted to tell people. See if you can find out when Isaiah did this.

Zechariah had said that the Messiah would ride into Jerusalem on a donkey. This is exactly what Jesus did. He rode into Jerusalem as a humble, peaceful leader, on the back of a donkey.

> **Psalm 118:26–27**
>
> **Blessed is He who comes in the name of the Lord.**
> **We bless you from the house of the Lord.**
> **The Lord is God.**
> **He has given us light.**
> **Carry branches in the festival procession.**

JESUS ARRIVES IN JERUSALEM

Many people expected the Messiah to be a great fighter. Any military leader would have been expected to arrive in Jerusalem on a war horse. By choosing a donkey, Jesus fulfilled the prophecies, and also showed that he was not a military leader.

C Jesus entering Jerusalem on a donkey

ARRANGEMENTS ARE MADE

Look carefully at the arrangements which seem to have been made. It seems as though Jesus had already made the plans, and the password was 'The Lord needs it' (Mark 11:1–11).

As Jesus rode from the Mount of Olives into the city, people scattered palm branches in front of him, and shouted out a welcome: 'Blessed is He who comes in the name of the Lord'.

At about this time each year, there was a festival called the **'Feast of Dedication'**. At this festival, people carried palm branches to the Temple. On the way, they sang Psalm 118. Look at the box on this page to find a verse from this Psalm. Can you see how it fits in with the way in which people greeted Jesus?

When **pilgrims** arrived in Jerusalem for this festival, they were often greeted with the words, 'Blessed is He who comes in the name of the Lord', and palm branches were waved before them. The people were therefore ready to give a rapturous welcome to the son of David.

NOTES/DATABASE

Use the glossary to look up the meanings of the following words. Then use the definitions to make your own notes or suitable entries on your database.

Passion Narrative	Pilgrim
Resurrection	Holy Week
Feast of Dedication	

ACTIVITIES

1 Quick quiz

You will need to have read the information in this unit as well as Mark 11:1–11 to help you answer these questions.

a What do we call the day when Jesus rode into Jerusalem on a donkey?

b What do we call the account of Jesus' last week in Jerusalem?

c What arrangements had Jesus already made?

d What did the people wave?

e What did they shout as Jesus went by?

2 Choose one of the two quotations on the previous page.

Look at the picture of the scrolls of the Torah in unit 7. Now make a miniature scroll using the quotation you have chosen.

Did you know?
Jewish people have miniature scrolls in little boxes on their doorposts. They are called Mezuzah.

Did you know?
Hebrew is written from right to left. The big letters are all consonants, and the dots are vowels.

Look at the Hebrew writing on this page, it is Psalm 118.

THE KING ARRIVES!

FURTHER ACTIVITIES

JERUSALEM WELCOMES JESUS, or THE DAY THE CROWD WENT BANANAS!

1 Design your own questionnaire, similar to this one.

2 Jesus was the most famous celebrity in Israel.

How do you think the crowd behaved on this occasion, when he rode into Jerusalem?

3 Look back at unit 1 to help you solve this problem.

NAME ....

AGE ....

1. Who is your favourite pop star?

....

2. What is your favourite football team? ....

3. Do you support any other team?   YES/NO

4. Do you watch your team play? YES/NO

5. Do you buy your favourite pop star's records?   YES/NO

6. Would you travel ten miles to see your team play?   YES/NO

7. Would you travel ten miles to see your favourite pop star? YES/NO

8. How would you describe the behaviour of the crowd when your team won the FA Cup? ....

....

9. How would you describe the behaviour of the crowd when your favourite star came to open a supermarket?

....

....

Now for some questions to make you really think!

4 Write down **two** ways in which Jesus fulfilled prophecies by riding into Jerusalem on a donkey.

5 a Design a collage showing Jesus' ride into Jerusalem. Odd pieces of fabric, or old magazines, could provide useful materials for this.

b If you have a computer and video digitizer, as well as the videos:
   'Jesus of Nazareth' (OUP)
   'Jesus' (International Films)
   'Jesus Christ Superstar' (Universal Pictures)
digitize some of the scenes from these films to form a wall display. Smaller versions of the same pictures would be good illustrations for your own written work.

Why did they call Jesus 'Son of David'?

6 a What is the Pope doing in this picture?

b Why do you think he is doing this?

c Draw a chart of the similarities and differences between the way in which the Pope arrives in a different country, and the way in which Jesus arrived in Jerusalem.

d What do you think Jesus would have said if he had seen the Pope kissing the ground in this way?

D The Pope arriving in Switzerland

7 Using information from earlier units, as well as this one, copy and complete the chart.

A The kind of Messiah the people expected	B What the Old Testament tells us about the Messiah	C The kind of Messiah Jesus showed himself to be

8 Write a story, based on Mark 11:1–17, which begins:
'I saw a crowd of people waving palm branches and shouting out with excitement. I went over to join them to find out the reason for the excitement. It was . . .'
Include illustrations.

9 Begin keeping a diary of '**Holy Week**' as we call Jesus' last week in Jerusalem before the Crucifixion.

Imagine you are one of the disciples and make appropriate diary entries for each day. The next four units will also help you.

DIARY

Sunday
    Today was the most marvellous day. At last Jesus is admitting that he is the Messiah. He had arranged for us to collect the donkey. We had to explain to the owner that "The Lord needs it". Then we took it back to Jesus on the Mount of Olives and he rode it in to Jerusalem. It was fantastic — the crowds went bananas!

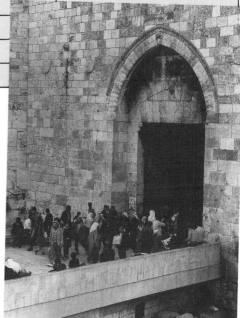

E Damascus gate

THROWING THE TRADERS OUT OF THE TEMPLE

After Jesus arrived in Jerusalem, he went straight to the **Temple**. The courtyards were crowded with traders, buying and selling. Jesus was angry at what he saw. There were people selling doves for worshippers to **sacrifice** in the Temple. Money changers haggled over the rate of exchange. Jesus threw the money changers out of the Temple, and overturned the stalls where people were selling doves. Although the official money was Roman money, the Temple authorities thought it was wrong to use Roman money. So everyone had to change their money into Shekels (special Jewish temple money).

Jesus stayed with his friends at Bethany. Each day he walked into Jerusalem. He went to the Temple where he taught anyone who wanted to listen about God and the way God wanted people to behave.

THE PARABLE OF THE VINEYARD

One day, Jesus told a parable about a man who owned a vineyard. After building a wall around the vineyard the owner went away on a journey. At harvest time, the owner sent servants to collect his share. The people who had been left in charge of the vineyard killed them. Finally the owner sent his son. They killed him too. Jesus meant that the owner was God, the servants were the prophets, and Jesus himself was the son. It was one more way of teaching his followers about what was going to happen to him (Matthew 21:33–44).

THE LAST SUPPER

Jesus had already made arrangements for the **Passover** meal. He sent his disciples ahead to prepare the room. You can find

A Jesus teaching in the Temple

out what the plans were which Jesus had made by reading Mark 14:12–16.

A large upstairs room had been set aside for Jesus and his disciples to eat the Passover meal. This meal is called **Seder** by Jewish people, and they still celebrate this festival meal each year. Jesus ate the Passover meal on Mount Zion. Nearby is the tomb of King David, who was an ancestor of Jesus. It was the custom for a Rabbi to eat the Passover meal near a spot associated with one of his ancestors. By choosing a room near to the tomb of King David, Jesus fitted in with this tradition.

In the time of Jesus it was thought to be polite to wash guests' feet when they arrived. The disciples could not agree whose job this should be, and so Jesus himself wrapped a towel around his waist and washed everyone's feet. Read the whole story in John 13: 1–17.

During the meal, Jesus told the disciples that one of them was about to betray him. He did not name Judas, but

B A Jewish market stall

told John and Peter that it would be the person who dipped his bread into the lamb stew at the same time as he did. Judas did this, and then left the feast.

Passover celebrates the time when God led the people of Israel (the Jews) out of slavery in Egypt and into the Promised Land. On that night, they ate special food which included lamb, bitter herbs and **unleavened** bread, and drank four cups of wine. It reminded them of slavery in Egypt and the power of God which brought them back to Israel.

After Jewish worship, they often have a little extra meal called a **Kiddush**, or a 'blessing'. After supper, Jesus took the bread and said 'This is my body', after he had blessed and broken it. 'This is my blood which is poured out for many, and which seals God's covenant with you', he said as he blessed the wine, and gave it to them to drink. He went on to say, 'I shall never drink wine again until I drink it afresh in the Kingdom of God'

Christians remember this event as the Last Supper. It is re-enacted in many Christian churches each Sunday and is called '**Mass**', '**Holy Communion**', 'The **Eucharist**' or 'The **Lord's Supper**'

NOTES/DATABASE

Use the glossary to look up the meanings of the following words. Then use the definitions to make your own notes or suitable entries on your database.

Temple	Christians
Sacrifice	Mass
Passover	Holy Communion
Seder	Eucharist
Unleavened bread	Lord's Supper

ACTIVITIES

Discuss

1 Many churches and cathedrals in this country and abroad need the extra money brought in by tourists to keep the building in good repair.

a Do you think that local groups of Christians should have to pay for the upkeep of buildings which are visited and enjoyed by many other people?

b What methods can you think of for raising money for the upkeep of buildings?

C Cathedral shop selling religious souvenirs

c Do you think that Jesus would be pleased that Christians spend so much time and money looking after buildings? Discuss the reasons for your answer.

Drama – The money changers are thrown out!

2 The class could be divided into four groups.

Group A could be responsible for the crowd in the Temple.

Group B could be the stage-hands, who need to look carefully at the small details. (Don't forget you'll need a lot of coins for the money changers.)

Group C – money changers/dove sellers.

Group D – Jesus and his disciples.

Within a short time you will be able to set the scene in the Temple and act out what happened. Work hard at developing what must have been an electric atmosphere.

3 Parable of the tenants in the vineyard

What is the correct caption for each picture?

a They killed the servants.

b The owner of the vineyard went to another country.

c He sent his servants to ask for his share of the harvest.

d He decided to send his own son.

4 Now write three more sentences which complete the story.

Make sure you use Mark 12:1–12.

BREAD AND WINE

THE PASSOVER

The last supper which Jesus had with his disciples was a Passover meal. Passover is a Jewish feast, celebrated in spring, when Jews remember that they were slaves in Egypt. They eat special food, including unleavened bread and red wine, as well as lamb. This helps them to remember that God led them out of Egypt into their own land.

FURTHER ACTIVITIES

The food you would find on a Seder dish.

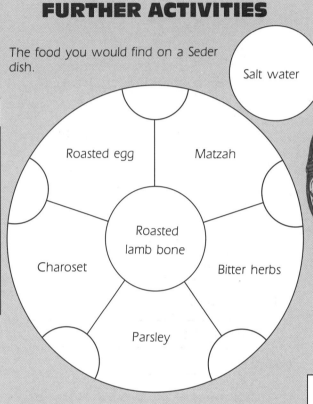

Salt water

Roasted egg

Matzah

Charoset

Roasted lamb bone

Bitter herbs

Parsley

D A decorated Seder dish

Food	Reason
Roasted egg	To show suffering.
Matzah (bread with no yeast)	To remind Jews that they had to leave Egypt in a hurry, so there was not enough time for the bread to rise.
Roasted lamb bone	To remember the lambs killed in Egypt the night before they left.
Bitter herbs	To show the bitterness of slavery.
Salt water	To show the tears of suffering.
Parsley	To remind Jews that the doorposts were marked with blood to show the angel of death which houses to pass over.
Charoset, a mixture of apples, spices, raisins and honey	To remind Jews that they had to make bricks when they were slaves in Egypt.
Four cups of wine	To remind Jews of the promises God gave to the people of Israel (Exodus 6:6–8).

A Jewish boy asks four questions about the Passover during the meal. The answers tell the Passover story.

E 'Why is this night different from all other nights?'

1 Imagine you are a member of a Jewish family and explain what would happen at a Passover meal. Also, explain to a stranger the meaning of the food, as well as the original event which is remembered at Passover.

Jesus of Nazareth welcomes you to a banquet to be held in his honour.

Paul wrote to the Corinthians to tell them about the Last Supper. Read I Corinthians II:23–25 to find out what he said.

2 Now try to answer these questions in your books:

a Which night was Paul telling the Corinthians about?

b What did the bread represent?

c What did the wine represent?

d What did Jesus want people to do to remember him?

3 Different names are used for the part of a service where people receive bread and wine.

Copy and complete the chart below, showing which of your local churches uses each name, and show its denomination. (Type of Church, e.g. Methodist.)

Name for bread and wine	Name of your local Church	Denomination
The breaking of bread		
The Eucharist		
The Holy Communion		
The Lord's Supper		
The Mass		

4 Study the pictures carefully, and complete the chart.

F Methodist: Communion

G Church of England: Eucharist

H Roman Catholic: Mass

I Greek Orthodox: Liturgy

Sharing the bread and the wine		
Church	**Similarities**	**Differences**

BETRAYAL

Judas had been looking for an opportunity to betray Jesus. He had already been to the chief priests, and they had promised him money if he helped them arrest Jesus (Mark 14:10–11).

During the **Passover** meal, Jesus made it clear that he knew all about Judas' plan to help the chief priests. Jesus sent Judas out from the feast with the words, 'What you have to do, do quickly!' (John 13:27).

After Judas had gone, Jesus gave his disciples a new rule to keep. 'Love one another', he said, 'as much as I love you' (John 13:34f). His followers would be known by the fact that they loved one another.

A Garden of Gethsemane

STAY AWAKE AND PRAY

Later, they left the room where they had eaten supper, and walked down **Mount Zion**, and along the Vale of Kidron until they came to the Garden of **Gethsemane**, where Jesus went away on his own to pray. He left Peter, James and John, asking them to stay awake and pray.

Jesus prayed that he should not have to suffer and die, if it were possible. He was, however, ready to do whatever God wanted him to do. When he returned to the disciples, he found them asleep. This happened three times altogether. On the third occasion, he told

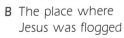

B The place where Jesus was flogged

them to get up and go with him as he was about to be betrayed (Matthew 26:36–46).

ARREST

Suddenly the peace of the Garden was disturbed. Armed guards had come with Judas, to arrest Jesus. Judas identified Jesus by kissing him. Jesus asked why it was necessary to arrest him at night, when he had been teaching in the Temple every day. The impetuous Peter was so furious that he cut off the ear of the **High Priest's** servant, which Jesus immediately healed.

The disciples scattered. Later, Peter crept after the guards as they led Jesus away to the house of Caiaphas, the High Priest, where he was imprisoned, and tried. Peter wanted to find out what was happening to Jesus, and he sat down with the guards.

TRIAL

The religious authorities tried to find witnesses who would testify against Jesus. None of them agreed with each other. Finally, he was asked, 'Are you the **Christ**, the Son of God?' When he replied that he was, he was attacked by the High Priest. His clothes were torn, and they told him he should die, because he was claiming to be equal with God. Some of them spat at him and he was blindfolded and hit. The guards then took him away and beat him (Mark 14:53–65).

I DON'T KNOW HIM

Peter was sitting outside in the courtyard. He was asked on three occasions whether he was one of Jesus' followers. Each time he said that he didn't even know him. The third time, a cock crowed, and Peter remembered what Jesus had said. 'Before the cock crows twice, you will disown me three times.' Peter ran away in tears (Mark 14:66–72).

he were her own son. Other women, who had followed Jesus from Galilee, watched from a distance.

At midday, a weird darkness covered the whole land. It lasted for three hours. Then at three o'clock, Jesus called out, 'My Father, my Father, why did you abandon me?' (Mark 15:34). 'It is completed' was Jesus' final cry (John 19:30).

The army officer in charge of the execution squad was so impressed by Jesus, that he said, 'This man really was the son of God'.

Jesus was already dead when the soldiers came to break the legs of the dying men. They did this to make them die more quickly. It wasn't necessary to break Jesus' legs, so they thrust a spear into his side instead.

BURIAL

The next day was the **Passover**. His friends had to act quickly to bury Jesus before Passover began. Joseph of Arimathea, a member of the Jewish religious Council, asked Pilate for the body of Jesus. He offered his own tomb to bury Jesus. They took the body down from the Cross, wrapped it in a linen sheet, and buried it hastily in this borrowed tomb. It seemed that all their hopes had come to nothing. Jesus had died.

NOTES/DATABASE

Use the glossary to look up the meanings of the following words. Then use the definitions to make your own notes or suitable entries on your database.

Crucifixion   Myrrh

Golgotha   Passover

ACTIVITIES

Where to find it

The Crucifixion

Matthew 27:27–56   Luke 23:26–49
Mark 15:16–41   John 19:16–30

C   Jesus being removed from the Cross

1 Quick quiz

a What happened if the prisoner died on the way to the crucifixion?

b Why did Simon of Cyrene carry Jesus' cross?

c How do you think Golgotha got its name?

d What did the label say which Pilate had placed on the cross?

e What were people who were crucified offered to dull the pain?

f Why do you think soldiers had to remain on guard?

g Why were the other two people crucified?

h How did Jesus arrange for his mother to be looked after?

i Why didn't the Romans break Jesus' legs; and what did they do instead?

j How was Jesus' burial arranged?

JESUS' WORDS FROM THE CROSS

'Forgive them, Father! They don't know what they are doing!' (Luke 23:34)
Jesus prays for the people who were responsible for his death.

'I promise you that today, you will be with me in paradise' (Luke 23:43)
Jesus made this promise to one of the criminals who was crucified with him.

'He is your son . . . she is your mother' (John 19:26–27)
Jesus asked John, his special friend, to take care of his mother.

'My God, my God, why have you forsaken me' (Mark 15:34)
Jesus quotes Psalm 22:1. A cry of loneliness and abandonment.

'I am thirsty' (John 19:28)
Jesus shows that he was completely human and felt physical pain like anyone else.

'It is completed' (John 19:30)
Jesus knows that he has completed the work God sent him to do.

'Father, into your hands, I place my spirit' (Luke 23:46)
The prayer of trust which every Jewish boy was taught to make each night, before he went to sleep.

2 Don't forget to keep your diary of Holy Week up to date!

Think about what you need to add from this unit.

FURTHER ACTIVITIES

What now?

After Jesus died, what did they all do?

How do you think his friends, and his enemies, felt?

1 Choose **four** of the people or groups of people from the circle below, and write down what you think their answer would have been to the question in the centre of the circle.

Look carefully at these pictures. They all tell us about the same event, the Crucifixion of Jesus.

2 Draw a four column chart, as shown opposite, and write down the similarities between the four photographs.

3 Repeat this, but this time show the differences.

D Mediaeval crucifixion

PETER was angry with himself because he had said three times that he did not know Jesus. Now, he perhaps felt, it was too late. He would never be able to make up for it.

MARY, Jesus' mother was very upset and shocked. She was cared for by John, and the other women.

JOSEPH OF ARIMATHEA, the Pharisee who gave his tomb to Jesus was possibly delighted that he had been able to show his support for Jesus at the end by giving his tomb.

BARABBAS was thrilled to be free, and planning his next attack on the Romans.

THE DISCIPLES were in hiding, probably scared that they might be arrested.

THE MOB of ordinary people who had shouted 'Crucify Him!' were probably upset and confused by what had happened.

'How do you feel now Jesus is dead?'

JUDAS was angry with himself over what he had done. He returned the money he had been given for betraying Jesus, then hanged himself.

HEROD, who hated rivals was probably glad that Jesus was dead.

JOHN, Jesus' closest friend was looking after Mary, Jesus' mother.

CAIAPHAS was delighted that he had managed to get rid of Jesus, but was worried that the body might be stolen so he was busy trying to organise a guard for the tomb.

THE WOMEN who had followed Jesus from Galilee were very upset, but keeping themselves busy by planning to put clean linen and spices on the body as soon as the Sabbath was over.

PILATE probably felt guilty because he knew he had made an innocent man die. He must also have been distressed because he had been forced to let Barabbas go free.

E Sixteenth century crucifixion

F Crucifixion
Salvador D

G Statue of Christ, Rio de Janeiro

Similarities between

D Mediaeval painting	E Sixteenth century painting	F Painting by Salvador Dali	G Carving

I Inside the Church of the Holy Sepulchre

J Golgotha – the place of the skull

For discussion

4 Why do you think the different artists chose to interpret the Crucifixion in their particular way?

5 Draw

You have discussed the interpretations made by each artist. Remembering these thoughts, try to draw your own interpretation of the Crucifixion.

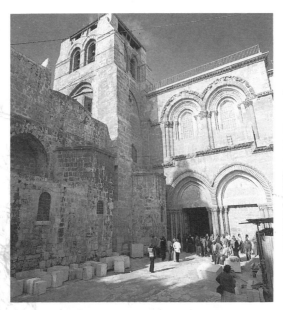

H Outside the Church of the Holy Sepulchre

K The garden tomb

WHERE DID THE CRUCIFIXION REALLY TAKE PLACE?

Was it site A?

or was it site B?

Let's find out what the evidence is in support of each site!

6 For which site do you think there is the most convincing evidence?

EVIDENCE FOR SITE A

Site A has been venerated since very early times as the place Jesus was crucified. There were still people alive then who could show where the Crucifixion happened. Not long after this, in fact by the third century, a Church was built on this site. The Bible says the Crucifixion and burial took place outside the walls of Jerusalem. This site was outside the walls of Jerusalem in the time of Jesus. Later on, the Crusaders in the twelfth century added to the Church.

EVIDENCE FOR SITE B

Gordon, in about 1860, was visiting Jerusalem. He was looking for the sites of the Crucifixion and burial. At that time, archaeologists had not yet discovered that the site of Jerusalem had changed. Therefore, he was looking outside the walls of Crusader Jerusalem. He found a first century rock-hewn tomb, in an old garden. There were shelves inside for the bodies, and a stone to roll over the entrance. The garden and the tomb itself fitted the Biblical description.

In Greek Orthodox Churches, on Easter morning, Christians greet each other with the joyful shout:

'Christ is Risen'

'He is Risen indeed!'

The event is called the **Resurrection**. 'Resurrection' means that after Jesus was crucified and buried, God brought him back to life. Jesus was seen by his followers, not just once, but over a period of several weeks. 'Resurrection' is the most important part of the Christian faith.

EYE WITNESSES

Each of the Gospel writers mentions the women who went to the tomb early on Sunday morning. They had been to the shops to buy spices and new linen to put on the body. When they found that Jesus was not in the tomb, they were very surprised. They had expected to find him there. Instead, they met two men, who told them that he had risen from the dead. Then, he appeared to Mary Magdalen, who was so bewildered at seeing him, that at first she thought he was the gardener!

There are a number of eye witness accounts of people who saw Jesus. They include Thomas, who was determined not to believe! He said that he would not believe unless he put his fingers into the holes which the nails made when Jesus was crucified. However, when Jesus offered him the chance to do that, even Thomas believed that Jesus was alive!

On one occasion, some of the disciples had gone fishing on the Sea of Galilee. They saw a man on the shore, who had lit a fire. When they realized that it was Jesus, Peter dived into the lake and swam ashore. Jesus had cooked their breakfast for them!

'Christ has died,

Christ is Risen

Christ will come again'

Many Christians use these words every Sunday at the Eucharist. The Resurrection is important for Christians.

46 C.E.

My dear Corinthians,

"I passed on to you what I received.... that Christ died for our sins.... that He was buried, and was raised to life on the third day. He appeared to Peter, and then to all twelve Apostles. Then He appeared to more than 500 of his followers all at once. Then He appeared to James, and then to all the Apostles. Last of all He appeared to me.

So, whether it came from me or from them, this is what we preach, and what you believe."

Your brother in Christ,

Paul of Tarsus.

A The garden tomb

If you find it difficult to believe in the Resurrection then it is important to answer this question:

WHAT HAPPENED TO THE BODY?

Here are some explanations which people have suggested in the past.

1 **Someone else was crucified.**
His mother was there, and talked with him, how could she possibly have made the mistake?

2 **He didn't really die.**
The Roman soldiers were experts in executing people. They made sure he was dead by thrusting a spear into his side.

3 **The women and the disciples visited the wrong tomb.**
Someone would very soon show the grieving family the right tomb!

4 **The authorities stole the body.**
They would have produced it very quickly when people began to say he was alive!

5 **The disciples stole the body.**
The disciples spent the rest of their lives telling the world that Jesus had risen from the dead. If it had not been true, would they have been prepared to suffer and die themselves?

There is not one single word or shred of evidence in history of any suggestion that anyone at all knew where Jesus' body had gone.

NOTES/DATABASE

Use the glossary to look up the meaning of the following word. Then use the definition to make your own notes or suitable entry on your database.

Resurrection

ACTIVITIES

1 Look up these Bible references and make a chart. Put the Bible reference in one column and fill in the event to which each refers in the second column.

Matthew	Event
Matthew 28:1–10	
Matthew 28:16–20	

Mark	Event
Mark 16:1–8	
Mark 16:9f	
Mark 16:12f	
Mark 16:14	

Luke	Event
Luke 24:1–12	
Luke 24:13–35	
Luke 24:36–53	

John	Event
John 20:1–10	
John 20:18–23	
John 20:24–29	
John 21:1–14	
John 21:15–24	

2 Now answer these questions:

a Write down the events which occur in all four Gospels.

b Which special story does Luke tell us about the Resurrection?

c Which special story does John tell us about the Resurrection?

CHRIST IS RISEN!

Person	Interview
 Mary Magdalen	
 Two disciples on the road to Emmaus	
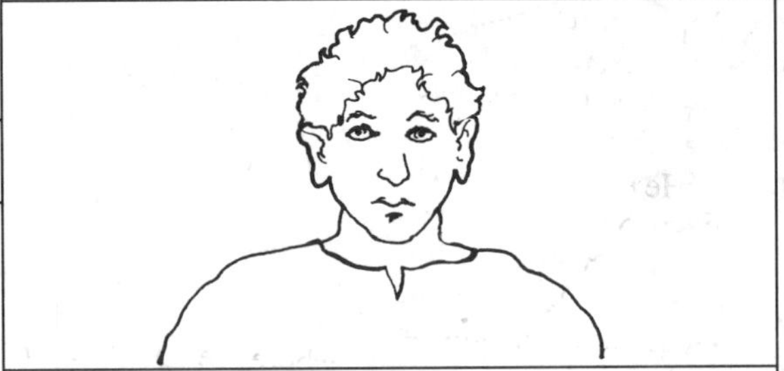 Thomas	
 The disciples who went fishing	

FURTHER ACTIVITIES

INTERVIEWS WITH EYE WITNESSES

Copy and complete the chart on the right.

1 Use the information from your chart of Gospel references to the Resurrection to help you write or record interviews with the people in the pictures.

THE DIFFERENCE THE RESURRECTION MAKES

Christians are people who believe that Jesus came back to life again after he had been killed on the Cross.

Many other people believe that Jesus was a great teacher, who showed people important things about how to live life unselfishly.

Holy Week Diary

You should now have a lot of things to write in your Holy Week diary. Make sure you have completed it!

INTERVIEWERS REQUIRED!

2 Your group are the producers of a programme for Radio Jerusalem. Your task is to produce an in-depth report of the events in Jerusalem in the last week of Jesus' life.

The Resurrection is rumoured. You will need to interview some of the eye witnesses. It will also be necessary to present the opposite view by interviewing a member of the Jewish authorities, and it could

be a good idea to interview the Roman soldier who checked to see whether Jesus was dead.

When you have worked out your report, use a tape recorder to record it.

JERUSALEM TIMES

SPECIAL PASSOVER EDITION

Passover 28 CE

HAVE YOU SEEN THIS MAN?

Reports have been reaching us here at the offices of the *Jerusalem Times*, that this man has been seen ALIVE! This is a picture of the notorious rabble rouser JESUS OF NAZARETH. He was crucified here in Jerusalem last week, accused of calling himself KING OF THE JEWS. He made staggering claims for himself, saying that he could rebuild the Temple (which has taken 70 years to build) in three days!

Now, his friends, a disreputable bunch from Galilee, are claiming that he is alive. Returned from the dead, they say, and alive and well!

He had been buried in a borrowed grave, which was found to be empty three days later when his family went to anoint the body.

Early on Sunday morning, it is alleged, he appeared to a reformed prostitute named Mary Magdalen, a well known figure in Jerusalem. She claims that she has seen him alive, but, we are bound to ask, can we treat her as a reliable witness?

Later, two men walking to Emmaus claim to have seen Jesus, although they admit they did not recognize him at first. They were on their way to the pub. No doubt you will be wondering whether they had visited the pub first!

Possibly a more reliable witness is Thomas. Admittedly he was a friend of Jesus, but he is not likely to have been misled. He said that unless he saw the marks of the nails, and the hole where the spear struck, he would not believe . . . but now even he is supporting this extraordinary tale!

Contact the *Jerusalem Times* if you think you have seen this man.

3 Letter to the editor

Write your letter to the editor in answer to the above newspaper article. Explain your views about what happened.

4 Group work

Design a booklet for 5–7 year olds which tells some of the Resurrection stories.

Decide which stories you wish to use. Decide which pictures you need. Delegate the production of the pictures to various members of the group. You will need some simple text to go with each of the pictures to explain the story. Make sure it really fits with the picture.

When you have written the text in rough, use the Desk Top Publishing System on the computer to print your text, or present it carefully in a booklet.

5 Discussion

Do you think that it would be possible to be a Christian without believing in the Resurrection of Jesus?

Another part of Christian belief is in life after death for everyone who believes in Jesus.

Do you think that believing in life after death would make any difference to the way in which Christians live their lives now?

6 Group work

You have been given the job of making a new documentary about the life of Jesus for a television company.

WANTED ARTISTS AND WRITERS

Work out:

a How you would set about the task.

b What evidence would you use?

You will need to decide whether there are any primary sources which you can use, and what secondary sources you will find helpful.

Some Christians say that the best evidence for the Resurrection of Jesus is the changed lives of Christians now. It might be a useful part of your documentary to interview some modern day Christians and find out what they believe about the Resurrection.

Good luck with the documentary! If you are fortunate enough to have a video camera you might like to video the documentary, or you could produce it on an audio tape.

NEW JOBS

After the Resurrection Jesus told the eleven **disciples** to meet him at a mountain in Galilee. He gave them new work to do, telling the world about him (Matthew 28:19–20).

THE ASCENSION

After Jesus had been with his followers for about forty days, the time came for him to return to his Father in Heaven. There needed to be a definite moment when they saw him go. Luke tells the story like this:

'When he had led them to a place near to Bethany, he lifted up his hands and Blessed them. While he was blessing them, he left them and was taken up into heaven. Then they worshipped him, and joyfully returned to Jerusalem. They were continually in the Temple, praising God' (Luke 24:50–53).

Luke wrote his **Gospel**, but he also wrote another book, called the Acts of the **Apostles**. This tells the story of what happened to the disciples after Jesus had gone back to heaven. Their new job was to tell the world about Jesus. The Acts of the Apostles is a record of how they began to do this.

Luke began by telling Theophilus, the person he was writing the book for,

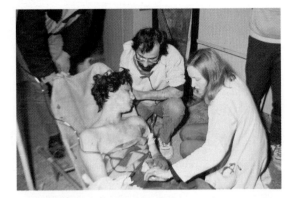

B Dr Pauline Cutting in Beirut

about the **Ascension**. It was the last thing which he mentioned in the Gospel, and the first thing which he mentions in Acts, where it is told in more detail. Acts 1:4–11 explains what happened.

PROMISE OF THE SPIRIT

Jesus promised the disciples a special gift. They had to wait in Jerusalem and, in a few days' time, they would receive the gift. Jesus reminded them that John the Baptist had **baptized** people using water, but now they were going to be baptized with the **Holy Spirit**. (Look carefully at Acts 1:4f and compare this with Mark 1:8.)

The disciples still hoped for the kind of Messiah who would be a military leader, or who could miraculously free Israel from the Romans, so they asked Jesus, 'Lord, are you going to restore the kingdom to Israel now?' (Acts 1:6). Read

A Christ the King, Rio de Janeiro

C A happy crowd

Jesus' reply very carefully, 'It's not your business to know the times and dates which God has decided. He has power over those. But you are going to have a special power when the Holy Spirit comes to you. Then you will tell people about me, in Jerusalem, in Judea, Samaria, and all over the world'.

These were Jesus' last words to the disciples, and he was immediately taken up into heaven. Luke says it was in a cloud. The cloud, to the Jewish people, showed that God was really present.

There was a special reason why the disciples were to receive the gift of the Holy Spirit. It was to help them in the new work which Jesus gave them of telling the whole world about him. When they received the Holy Spirit, they would know, all the time, that Jesus was really with them, and helping them in everything that they did.

NOTES/DATABASE

Use the glossary to look up the meanings of the following words. Then use the definitions to make your own notes or suitable entries on your database.

Disciple	Ascension
Gospel	Baptized
Apostle	Holy Spirit

Christ has died
Christ is Risen
Christ will come again.

'He ascended into heaven, and is seated at the right hand of the Father'

He will come again in glory.

ACTIVITIES

1 **Quick quiz**

a What was the job which Jesus gave the disciples to do?

b Why were there only eleven disciples?

c How long was Jesus with his followers after the Resurrection?

d Where did Jesus take the disciples just before he returned to heaven?

e How would you describe the disciples' mood when they returned to Jerusalem?

f What are the names of the two books which Luke wrote?

g What does the 'Acts of the Apostles' tell us about?

h Who was Luke writing the books for?

i Why did Jesus tell the disciples to wait in Jerusalem?

j What was the question which the disciples asked Jesus?

k Where did Jesus tell the disciples that they would tell the people about him?

l What difference do you think that the gift of the Holy Spirit would make to the disciples?

2 a Do you think that a picture like the one on the right helps people to understand what it means to say that Jesus is in heaven? Write down some reasons for your choice.

b Explain how the picture on the right fits in with the Christian beliefs in the above quotations.

c Look at the picture of 'Christo Rei' or 'Christ the King'. It looks as though Jesus is blessing the city of Rio de Janeiro. How far do you think this helps people to understand why Jesus had to return to heaven?

3 Imagine that you are leaving your school and moving to a different part of the country:

a How would you feel?

b How would your best friend feel?

c If your best friend moved away and you knew you wouldn't see her again, what kind of things would you each do to show you cared about each other? Make a list.

d The disciples' best friend was Jesus. He left them. How do you think they felt? (Luke 24:52). Why do you think they felt like this?

INTRODUCING LUKE

Luke wrote a Life of Jesus, which we call the Gospel, and a book called the Acts of the Apostles. He was a very careful historian. He wanted to make sure that his information was accurate. He went with Paul on some of his journeys, and wrote about the adventures which they had together. Even when Paul was in prison, Luke was with him. When they went to Israel, Luke must have spent some time travelling around and talking to the people who knew Jesus when he was on earth, and Luke put those stories in his Gospel. He was specially interested in the way Jesus treated poor people and women, and people who were thought to be of little value, as well as in people who were not Jews. He wrote the Gospel and the Acts of the Apostles to encourage people who were not Jews to believe in Jesus. It seems likely that he was a doctor, and almost certainly a Greek. He wrote a very accurate and vivid account of the life of the early Christians, and of the lives and work of both Peter and Paul. In some parts of the Acts of the Apostles he writes it from his own point of view. It often says 'we did' something.

SUCCESSOR FOR JUDAS

Read Acts 1:12–26 to find out how the disciples chose a successor for Judas.

FURTHER ACTIVITIES

1 Design and complete a passport application form for Dr. Luke.

PASSPORT APPLICATION

Name ___Luke___

Nationality ___Greek___

Year of birth ___? 14 C.E.___

Status (delete as necessary)
former SLAVE
~~FREEMAN~~
~~FREEBORN~~
~~ROMAN CITIZEN~~

a) If FREEMAN give date when slavery was ended and name of person who freed slave
___PAUL OF TARSUS , 36 C.E.___

b) If ROMAN CITIZEN state date purchased or citizen by birth ___N/A.___

Occupation ___Doctor___

Published works ___Life of Jesus___

Any other information ___Companion of Paul of Tarsus, interested in welfare of slaves, women and underprivileged; history one of my important interests.___

Address to which passport would be sent
___19, Acropolis Way,___
___Athens,___
___Greece.___

Reason for visit
___to collect information for my new book on the lives of Peter and Paul of Tarsus.___

2 Test yourself

Answer these questions in complete sentences.

a What country did Luke come from?

b What was his job?

c Who did he travel with?

d What were the two books which he wrote?

e How do you think he collected the information for his book about the life of Jesus?

f Look at Acts 1:1. Who did he write the books for?

g What kind of people was he specially interested in?

h Why do you think that Luke wanted people who were not Jews to read his books?

i How do we know that Luke was sometimes writing about events in which he actually took part?

j Luke's writings are what we call 'primary sources' because he wrote about events which he saw himself. Do you think that this makes them a reliable source of information? Write down some reasons for your answer.

POST VACANT
URGENT
APOSTLE NEEDED NOW
Apply in writing to:
The Upstairs Room,
Mount Zion,
Near The Tomb of King David,
Jerusalem.
Following the death of Judas, this vital job has now become vacant, and requires someone with very special qualities.

DIFFERENT WAYS OF TAKING A DECISION

3 Imagine you are Matthias.

You decide to apply for the job in the advert. Write a letter to the Apostles. You need to include:

a your qualifications;

b why you wish to apply for this demanding post;

c why you are the best person for them to choose;

d any extra interesting information which may help them to decide to choose you.

4 Now imagine you are one of the Apostles.

a You have just received several letters from people who have applied for Judas' job. You and your friends are all sitting around looking at the letters trying to decide who is the best person for the job. Naturally, there are lots of different opinions. Make a list of all the qualities you are looking for in the application letters. (Reading Acts 1:20b–26 may well help you.)

b What different ways of taking decisions are shown in the three pictures on this page?

c Are any of these similar to the way the Apostles decided on a replacement for Judas?

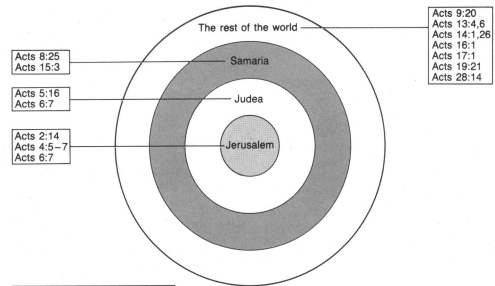

The rest of the world

Samaria

Judea

Jerusalem

| Acts 9:20 |
| Acts 13:4,6 |
| Acts 14:1,26 |
| Acts 16:1 |
| Acts 17:1 |
| Acts 19:21 |
| Acts 28:14 |

| Acts 8:25 |
| Acts 15:3 |

| Acts 5:16 |
| Acts 6:7 |

| Acts 2:14 |
| Acts 4:5–7 |
| Acts 6:7 |

'You will tell people about me in Jerusalem, in Judea and Samaria, and throughout the rest of the world.'

5 Look up the Bible references at the end of each string, and write down how that verse helps to show that Acts 1:8 came true.

6 Make a list of the places you have found where the Apostles told other people about Jesus.

You might like to see if you can find them on a map.

Rome was the most important city in the world at that time.

Why do you think Luke chose to end his book when Paul was telling people in Rome about Jesus?

THE FEAST OF PENTECOST

Jerusalem was crowded with people who had come from all over the world to enjoy the **Feast of Pentecost**. During Pentecost, Jews everywhere remembered the time when, hundreds of years earlier, God had given them a very special gift. This special gift was the two stones with the Ten Commandments written on them. God gave these to Moses, on the top of Mount Sinai. Jews were proud of the fact that they were the only nation to have a God who gave them a clear set of rules to help them to live their lives the way God wanted them to.

WAITING FOR A GIFT FROM GOD

The followers of Jesus were waiting now for another gift. In the Old Testament it said that after the **Messiah** came, the Law (Ten Commandments) would not be written on stones, but God would write it directly into men's hearts and minds (Jeremiah 31:33). This is what the disciples were now waiting for. When the Holy Spirit came to them, they would know what God wanted them to do.

THE SPIRIT COMES

In the Old Testament, fire and wind are signs which show that God is really present. (Elijah in I Kings 19 was really surprised that God was not in the wind or fire.) Jesus' followers were shown that God was really with them by the fire and wind. It was a way that they could understand God's presence. They were filled with a deep sense of joy because they knew that God was really with them.

The **disciples** were so excited that people outside began to gather round, to find out what was happening. To their

A 'They came from all over the world'

amazement, everyone who was there could hear the disciples in their own language. It didn't matter where in the world they came from, or what their native language was, everyone understood them clearly.

Some of the crowd thought they were drunk, because they all seemed so excited. However, Peter quickly explained that they weren't drunk. It was, he said, only nine o'clock in the morning, how could they be? But, he said, they were filled instead with the Holy Spirit, just as the **prophet** Joel, in the Old Testament, had promised.

This is what Joel said:
'God says,
I will pour out my spirit on all people.
Your sons and daughters will prophesy,
your young men will see visions and your old men will dream dreams.
I will pour out my spirit on all my servants, young and old, men and women'

Peter went on to tell the crowd about Jesus. Read Acts 2:22–24 carefully to find out what he said.

NEW BELIEVERS

Soon many of the crowd wanted to know what to do to have the same special relationship with God through the Holy Spirit which Peter and the other disciples had. So Peter told them, 'Be really sorry for what you have done wrong, believe in Jesus, and be **baptized**, and the Holy Spirit will come to you as well' (Acts 2:38). That day, three thousand people became believers in Jesus. They weren't only from Jerusalem. They were from all over the world. When they went back to their own countries, they would be able to tell people there about Jesus, because they had each heard the message about Jesus in their own language.

B 'He will baptize with the Holy Spirit and with fire' (Matthew 3:11)

ACTIVITIES

1 **Quick quiz**

a Why was Jerusalem crowded with people?

b What was the Jewish name for the festival?

c What did the Jews celebrate at this festival?

d Why were the Jews proud of their law?

e What were the disciples waiting for?

f What were the signs which showed the disciples that God was really with them?

g Why did a crowd gather?

h What language did each person in the crowd hear the disciples speak in?

i How did Peter explain that they weren't drunk?

j What did Peter tell the people in the crowd that they had to do if they wanted the Holy Spirit as well?

k How many people became believers in Jesus that day?

l Why do you think that God chose this particular day to give the disciples this special gift?

Map work

2 Copy the map into your book, and mark on it clearly the places from which people came to Jerusalem for the Feast of Pentecost.

Remember. These are all places where there would soon be groups of Christians, as those who had heard Peter speaking returned to their own countries and told other people about Jesus.

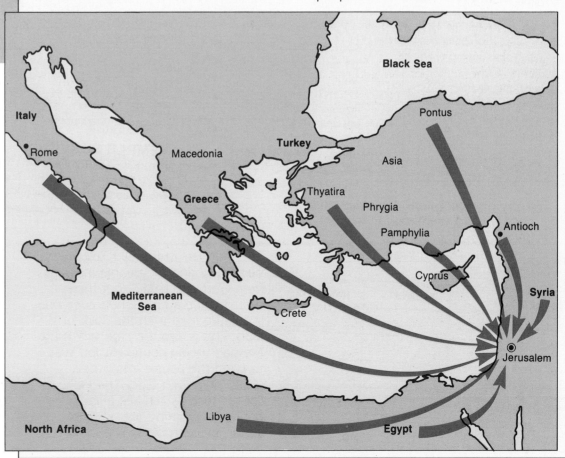

FURTHER ACTIVITIES

JERUSALEM TODAY

SPECIAL EDITION FOR PENTECOST

DRUNK AT DAWN?

Jerusalem was shaken this morning by noisy followers of Jesus of Nazareth, the Galilean rebel who was executed recently. For some weeks, his followers have claimed that he was alive. Now, they claim that he has given them the gift of the Holy Spirit, which the prophets said would be given to Israel when the Messiah came. They have, of course, been saying that their dead rabbi was none other than the Messiah himself. Quoting the prophet Joel, Peter told a crowd of over three thousand people that Jesus had filled his followers with the Holy Spirit. Those who were there said that the group of Followers of the Way, as they now call themselves, were behaving exactly like a lot of drunks. To defend himself, Peter told the crowd that they couldn't be drunk as it was only nine o'clock in the morning, and the pubs weren't open yet.

Mass baptisms at pool of Siloam

Following Peter's extravagant claims for his dead leader, many people wanted to join the former disciples of Jesus. Peter told them to be baptized. Apparently, over three thousand people have become baptized followers of this Jesus. The religious authorities were not available for comment today, but are widely believed to be opposed to any baptism of Jews. Baptism, they say, is only for people who were not born Jews.

TEMPLE SERVICES

Led this week by Caiaphas, the High Priest. 12 a.m. Readings from Prophets, Animal Sacrifices.

1 Important events are always reported by all the different newspapers.

They often take slightly different points of view.

Imagine you are a reporter from a different Jerusalem newspaper and design your own front cover reporting this story.

What does the Old Testament say about the Holy Spirit?

The 'Spirit' of God is mentioned right at the beginning of the Bible. Genesis 1:2 says that the Spirit was present at the creation of the world.

Some people in the Old Testament are said to have been given the Spirit of God for different reasons.

2 Copy and complete this chart of people who were said to have been given the Spirit of God, giving the reason why they needed it.

Reference	Name	Reason
Exodus 31:3		
Numbers 11:25		
1 Samuel 10:10		
1 Samuel 16:13		
Isaiah 11:2		

The prophets in the Old Testament began to bring the people messages from God which said that there would come a time when everyone would be filled with the Spirit of God. This is also the time when the Messiah would come. His job was to bring the people into a new relationship with God. The Holy Spirit is seen as actually being poured out, almost like a jug of water, over people. It is also seen as

'Unless you are born of water and the Holy Spirit, you cannot enter the Kingdom of Heaven.' John 3:5

God living within a person, to lead and guide and help them to live the way God wanted them to.

3 Copy the chart below, look up the references and place a tick in the correct column.

Reference	Poured out on someone	Living within someone
Psalm 51:11		
Isaiah 32:15		
Isaiah 44:3		
Isaiah 61:1		
Ezekiel 11:19		
Ezekiel 36:26		
Joel 2:28		

The 'Spirit of God', or 'The Holy Spirit', was not, therefore, a new idea to those people who heard Peter speak on the Feast of Pentecost. It was something which the prophets had promised in the Old Testament. John the Baptist said that the Messiah would baptize with the Holy Spirit (Mark 1:8). Jesus promised the Holy Spirit to everyone who believed in him.

The people in Jerusalem knew about the Holy Spirit. It is not surprising that they wanted to be filled with the Holy Spirit. It was the fulfilment of the promises of the Old Testament, and to the Jewish listener at the time, it was proof that Jesus really was the Messiah.

THE DIFFERENCE THE SPIRIT MADE

What do you think life was like in the early Church?

4 a Read Acts 42–47.

   Draw the picture of 'The Church in Jerusalem'.

   Use verse 42 to find four things which the believers did. Place each one under the correct picture.

b Make a list of the sort of things that you are likely to share with your brother or sister.

c Write a few sentences about the way in which you share things at school.

d Read verses 44–45 again, and then explain how the first believers shared things with each other.

e Read Acts 3:1–9.
   Now make several drawings in your book, to illustrate what you have read. This is an ideal occasion to draw a cartoon strip!

f Look in Acts 5:12–16.
   This will have told you about the other occasions on which people were healed. Write a short story about these events.

g Read Acts 5:17 and 18.
   Write a few sentences explaining what had happened to the Apostles.

h Read Acts 5:19–25.
   Now you can write a conversation in which you have to explain to the Sadducees (who had arrested the Apostles) why the Apostles are teaching in the Temple when they should have been in prison!

APOSTLES

The disciples began to do the new work which Jesus had given them. People started to call them **'Apostles'** instead of disciples. This means someone who is 'sent out with a job to do'.

People in Jerusalem were impressed by the way that Jesus' followers shared their possessions and made sure that everyone was properly looked after. Every day, more people became followers of Jesus. Soon there were more than five thousand people in Jerusalem who believed in Jesus.

Sometimes people sold their extra belongings and gave the money to the Apostles. They used it to help other people so that there was no one who was hungry or without a home.

A Food distribution in Calcutta

The Apostles realized that they were spending so much time looking after people and sharing things out equally that they had no time left to do the job which Jesus had given them. Greek speaking believers who were widows, and very poor, began to complain that the Hebrew speaking widows were getting bigger shares of food than they were. The Apostles decided that they needed some extra help (Acts 6:1–4).

CHOOSING THE DEACONS

The Apostles decided to choose seven men to be **deacons**. Their job would be to help people share their possessions so that everyone was like a brother or sister to everyone else. It was the Greek speaking women who had complained, so the people that were chosen for the job were people who had Greek names. You can find a list of their names in Acts 6:5. One of them, who was called Nicholas, was from Antioch. He was mentioned specially because he was not a Jew, but a convert to **Judaism**.

When the deacons had been chosen the Apostles 'laid hands on them'. This was a way of passing on to these men the authority which Jesus had given them. Today the Church still uses this method. When someone becomes a deacon or **priest** now, the **Bishop** places his hands on the person's head in a special service called **ordination**. This is to pass on the Church's authority to do the work which Jesus gave to the Apostles. (A Bishop has the same sort of position in the church now as the Apostles had then.)

All of the deacons were 'Full of the Spirit'. Look at the previous unit to make sure you understand what that means. People were given the Holy Spirit by Jesus so that they could tell other people about Jesus. Two of the deacons were especially good at this. Their names were Philip and Stephen.

NOTES/DATABASE

Use the glossary to look up the meanings of these words.
Then use the definitions to make your own notes or your own suitable entries on your database.

Apostles	Bishop
Deacon	Ordination
Judaism	Confirmation
Priest	

B An ordination

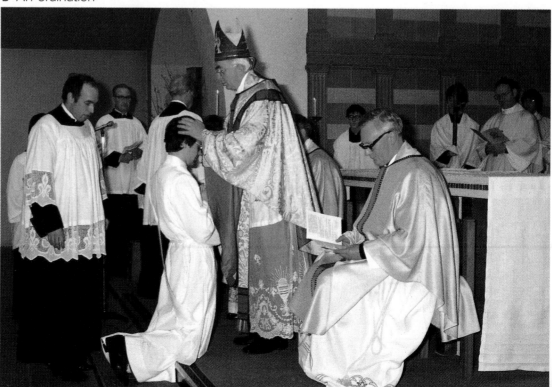

ACTIVITIES

Quick quiz

1 a What was the new name which the disciples had?

b Why do you think that they were called by this name?

c Why were they so busy?

d How many believers were there in Jerusalem now?

e Write down one way in which they got enough money to look after everyone.

f What did the Greek widows complain about?

g How did the Apostles get some extra help?

h Why do you think they chose Greek speaking men to be deacons?

i Why was Nicholas of Antioch specially mentioned?

j Why did the Apostles lay hands on the people who were chosen to be deacons?

k Who chose the deacons?

There are exactly the same reasons for the laying on of hands in the Church today as there were in New Testament times. The heading at the top of each of the four boxes is the name which is used in the Church now. Under it you will find a reason why someone in the Bible laid hands on someone else, and the place in the Bible where you would find that event.

2 a Look up each reference to find out what happened on each occasion mentioned here.

b Use the Glossary to make sure that you understand the meaning of ordination and **confirmation**.

c Copy the chart into your book, but instead of the words in the centre of each box, draw a picture which shows what the Bible reference was all about.

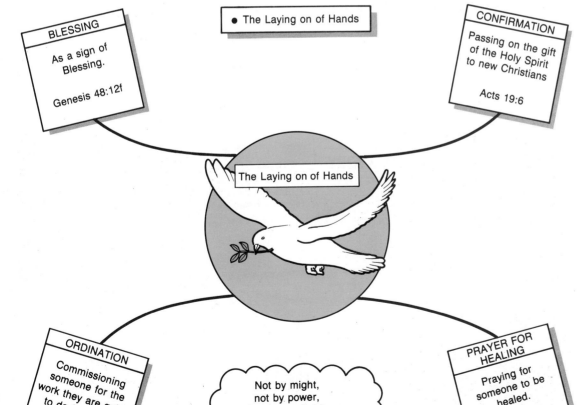

● The Laying on of Hands

BLESSING
As a sign of Blessing.
Genesis 48:12f

CONFIRMATION
Passing on the gift of the Holy Spirit to new Christians
Acts 19:6

The Laying on of Hands

ORDINATION
Commissioning someone for the work they are going to do for Jesus.
Acts 13:3

Not by might, not by power, but by my Spirit, says the Lord.
Zechariah 4:6

PRAYER FOR HEALING
Praying for someone to be healed.
Mark 16:15

MEET SOME CHRISTIANS!

3 Ask your teacher if it would be possible to invite a Vicar, Priest or Minister to come and tell you why he chose to serve Jesus in this particular way.

Try and find out whether the laying on of hands was a very special moment in his life. Discuss and write down what questions you would like to ask your visitors about the work they do.

4 Try and find someone near your own age who has been confirmed recently. Interview your friend to find out exactly what happened at the Confirmation. He or she may be able to bring some pictures to show the class.

FURTHER ACTIVITIES

MURDER!

A young man was stoned to death today, outside the offices of the Sanhedrin, the ruling council. Police investigating the incident are treating the death as MURDER..!

POLICE REPORT

Victim _____

Sex _____

Age _____

Date _____

Cause of death _____

Time of death _____

Eye witnesses _____

_____

_____

Suspects _____

_____

REWARD

WHERE WERE YOU WHEN THIS MAN WAS KILLED?

The parents of Stephen, the young man pictured here, are offering a substantial reward for any information which will help them discover who is responsible for the death of their son.

THEY FEAR THAT THE TRUTH IS BEING HUSHED UP!!!

CAN YOU HELP?

---

1 **The investigation continues**

You are the police officer conducting the investigation into the death of Stephen. This is a delicate investigation. Members of the Sanhedrin, the government, may be involved.

You need to know:
1 Who saw the killing.
2 Who to interview.
3 Why he was killed.
4 Who did it.

Use Acts 6:8–15 and Acts 7:51–8:2 to help you discover the facts behind the murder.

Then write your top secret report. Be careful not to leak any information to reporters. The whole affair is likely to be hushed up as it may involve members of the government.

UNDER SEALED ORDERS

ACTS 8:26–40   PHILIP'S STORY

Background

Philip was one of the deacons (see Acts 6:4). God had given him the special gift of being able to tell other people about Jesus. In Samaria crowds of people had listened very carefully to what Philip had to say about Jesus.

We join the story at the point where Philip is under sealed orders. He knows that God has a job for him, but he doesn't yet know what it is going to be.

Now read on!

PHILIP'S ASSIGNMENT

Heaven

You are to go into the desert near Gaza. There, you will meet an important man.

You will know him when you see him. He will be carrying something to help you recognise him.

You will be told what you have to do.

Transport will be provided for the return journey.

GOD

JESUS

Philip the Evangelist
SEALED ORDERS

PRIVATE AND CONFIDENTIAL

2 Your assignment

Your class are a film crew.

Nearly two thousand years later, your boss, the film director, heard the story of Philip's Mission Under Sealed Orders.

Your task is to make an exciting new video about this unique event.

Either

Organize a group to act this story for the rest of the class.

or

Involve everyone!
If you have a video camera available, make a video of this event.

People you will need:

a Script writers
b Actors
c Director
d Stage manager
e Graphic designers
f Film crew

Some people might like to design advertisements and a sleeve for your video. If you have a computer with a Desk Top Publishing System, you could use this to produce your advertising material.

You may also like to appoint reporters for the 'Premier' (the first time a film is shown). They will then need to write reviews of the video (for different newspapers, of course). These could also be printed on the Desk Top Publishing System.

If you have a video digitizer, you could also digitize some pictures from the video to include in your reviews and advertisements.

WHO'S NEEDED NOW?

Are you interested in what sort of openings there are for serving God in East Asia with the OMF?
Here are just some examples of the numbers we could use:

* **24 people to reach out to the fast increasing thousands of factory workers and to help start new churches in industrial zones in Taiwan.**
* **75 workers to help plant new churches in Japan.**
* **20 couples for evangelism in urban areas of the Philippines.**
* **18 couples to live and evangelize among Philippines' tribal people.**
* **20 couples to take up teaching and training opportunities in universities, theological colleges and churches in Indonesia.**

Other countries need workers too, such as Thailand where the priority is town and city evangelism. Individuals with a variety of gifts and skills, e.g. in medicine, in administration, in school teaching, are vital to make up the total body of the Fellowship as it works for the fastest possible spread of the gospel in East Asia.

Overseas Missionary Fellowship.

3 Read Acts 6:1–15, 54–59, and 8:26–40 again. Now look carefully at the advertisement.

a Make a list of the kind of things which Philip and Stephen did in the Early Church.

b What kind of things are the Overseas Missionary Fellowship (OMF) asking people to do?

c What similarities can you see between the work of the OMF and the work which the deacons did in the Early Church?

CHRISTIAN TEACHERS
Especially for R.E., Maths, Science, English and Commerce for Secondary Schools in Africa and Papua, New Guinea.
Voluntary terms – 2 year contracts.
Apply to:
Volunteer Missionary Movement, Shenley Lane, London Colney, St. Albans, Herts. AL2 1AR.
Tel: 0727 24853 (sae appreciated)
(41145)   Times Educational Supplement, 12.8.88

4 Look at the advertisement from the *Times Educational Supplement*.

a Where are teachers being asked to go?

b Why do you think there is a need for Christian teachers to teach subjects like maths and science as well as RE?

5 a What qualities do you think a person would need to answer one of these advertisements?

b If the Missionary Society had two people who had applied for the same job, but could only send one person, how do you think they might choose which person to send?

C Desmond Tutu

A Caesarea

One of the lessons which Peter had to learn was that Jesus came for everyone, and not just Jews. The news about Jesus was spreading very quickly. A Roman soldier called Cornelius had become interested in the Jewish faith, in One God. Although someone could become a '**God-fearer**' (someone who believed in the Jewish religion), he could never be truly part of the family of Jews.

B Roman port at Caesarea

The only way to be Jewish is by being born into a Jewish family.

Cornelius was a 'God-fearer'. He was generous and followed the Jewish faith in every way he could. One day, he was praying to God, and his prayers were answered in a rather unusual way. He was told to send messengers to a place called Joppa, to the house of a man called Simon the Tanner. A man was staying there called Peter. The messengers were to say that God had told Peter to come to Caesarea to talk to Cornelius.

PETER IN JOPPA

In Joppa, Peter was waiting for his dinner to be cooked. He went up on the roof to pray, and he began day dreaming.

He imagined that he saw a huge sheet, a bit like the sail of a boat, coming down out of the sky. In it were all sorts of animals which Jews were not allowed to eat. Peter heard a voice telling him to get up, and kill one of the animals and eat it. Peter reacted like any good Jew. 'Not likely!', he said. 'I'm a good Jew,

I've never eaten anything impure which was forbidden by Jewish Law!' Then Peter heard a voice which said, 'You must not call anything impure which God has made pure'. He didn't understand this. The same vision came three times.

Peter was still wondering what this meant when messengers arrived from Cornelius. The **Holy Spirit** told Peter that there were three men downstairs and Peter was to go with them.

PETER IN CAESAREA

The next day, Peter returned to Caesarea with the three men. Peter was obviously nervous about entering the house of someone who was not Jewish. Peter said that it was against the Jewish Law to visit the house of someone who wasn't a Jew. God had shown him that

Caesarea

Mediterranean Sea

SAMARIA

Joppa

JUDEA

he was not to think like this any more. God doesn't have favourites.

When Peter found out why Cornelius had sent for him, he started to tell Cornelius about Jesus and especially about the **Resurrection**. Read what Peter said in Acts 10:34–43. While Peter was still speaking, Cornelius and his family were all filled with the Holy Spirit in exactly the same way as Peter and the other disciples had been on the Day of **Pentecost**. The Jewish believers were amazed. It was unbelievable to them that God should fill people who were not Jews with the Holy Spirit.

Peter and the others had learned a valuable lesson. God accepts everyone who wants to believe in Him through Jesus, whatever nation they happen to belong to.

This was an important lesson for the Church to learn. By accepting **Gentiles** (people who are not Jews) on equal terms, the way was open for Christianity to spread beyond Israel, throughout the rest of the world.

NOTES/DATABASE

Use the glossary to look up the meanings of the following words. Then use the definitions to make your own notes or suitable entries on your database.

God-fearer	Pentecost
Holy Spirit	Gentile
Resurrection	Kosher

The Romans worshipped the Emperor . . .

. . . and lots of other gods

ACTIVITIES

1 **Quick quiz**

a Why did Jewish people believe they had a special relationship with God?

Why did God send prophets?

What was Roman religion like?

d What is a 'God-fearer'?

e What was the name of the Roman soldier who was a 'God-fearer'?

f How was his prayer answered?

g What was Peter doing in Joppa?

h What happened in Peter's dream?

i How did Peter know that there were three men waiting for him?

j What happened at Cornelius' house?

2 a Look in an encyclopaedia to find out the names of some Roman gods, and what each one was. Look under 'gods' as well as 'Roman'. It would be a good idea to display your results in a chart similar to the one below.

Name of God	Reason for worship
A Jupiter	Chief god
B	

b Why do you think the Emperor wanted to be worshipped like a god?

For discussion

3 Discuss why you think Romans would be attracted to the idea of only One God.

FURTHER ACTIVITIES

WHY PETER NEVER ATE RABBIT!

Things the Jews **can** eat: (Look in Leviticus 11 to see if you can find them.)

Any animals which have split hooves and chew the cud.

and many birds

even locusts

fish

THEY CAN'T EAT MEAT AND MILK/DAIRY FOODS IN THE SAME MEAL.

But the Jews **cannot** eat: (Look in Leviticus 11 again.)

✡

SOLOMON'S KOSHER FOOD

MENU

CHICKEN BLINTZ
SALT BEEF
LATKIS
LOXON PUDDING
BLACK COFFEE

Jewish food is called **kosher**. Jewish restaurants are called kosher restaurants.

1 a Why does Solomon only serve black coffee with this menu?

   b Could you order cheese and biscuits with this meal? Give reasons for your answer.

2 a Which animals do you think were in the sheet in Peter's vision?

   b Why had Peter never eaten this kind of meat?

   c Why do you think this vision helped Peter to understand that God wanted Gentiles to believe in Jesus as well?

3 Try to find a Jewish cookery book.

   Then work out your own menu for a special kosher meal. Remember you cannot mix dairy dishes with meat dishes.

   It might be possible to ask your teacher if you could cook a kosher meal.

PETER IS ASKED TO EXPLAIN

Acts 10:46b–48
'Then Peter said "Can anyone stop these people being baptized? They have received the Holy Spirit, just as we have." '

4 In pairs

Write a script for a chat show.

Imagine one of you is Peter and the other one is questioning him to find out two things:

a Why he ate with the Gentiles in their house;
and

b Why he baptized the whole family.

Also

c Write down the questions you should ask Peter;
and

d Write down the answers he would have made.

Now,

e If you can use a tape recorder, tape the question and answer session which Peter has in order to explain what he did.

Acts 11:18
'When they heard this, they had no further objections. They praised God and said "Gentiles can be believers in Jesus too".'

THE GREAT ESCAPE

5 Look carefully at Acts 12:1–19 and write a short caption for each picture.

6 Use your Bible.

All the answers are in Acts 12:1–19. Write out and complete these sentences in your book.

a King Herod II arrested them because ....
....

b James was ....
....

c Peter was guarded by ....
....

7 Now answer these questions.

a What was the Church doing while Peter was in prison?

b Do you think that it would have been easy to escape from this prison?

c What happened to the chains?

d What did Peter think was happening?

e How did the gate open?

f Where was Peter when the angel left him?

8 In your own words, describe what happened when Peter knocked on the door of Mary's house.

9 What do you think King Herod II said to the soldiers the next morning when they discovered Peter had gone?

SAUL

'I have chosen him to tell the **Gentiles** about me' (Acts 9:15). This is what God said about Saul of Tarsus. At the time it didn't seem very likely.

Saul – that's his Jewish name, was also known as Paul – that's his Greek name. He was born at Tarsus in what is now Turkey. He was a well educated young Jewish man, who was intending to become a **rabbi**. His family were proud to be able to trace their family tree right back to Benjamin, one of Jacob's sons, and through him to Abraham. They were quite rich, and Saul had in fact been born a Roman citizen. This was thought to be a great honour.

Every Jewish boy was brought up to have a trade, even if he was intending to be a rabbi, and young Saul was trained to be a tent maker, as well as attending the University. Later he was sent to Jerusalem to continue his training to become a rabbi. His teacher in Jerusalem was the **Pharisee** Gamaliel.

PERSECUTING THE CHRISTIANS

When Saul heard Christians praying to Jesus, and believing that Jesus was the Son of God, he was horrified. It seemed to him that they were no longer believing in only one God. He did not understand the Christian teaching that God the Father, and Jesus, and the Holy Spirit, were all One God.

Saul set out to make life difficult for people who believed in Jesus. This is called '**persecution**'. If captured, Christians were to be put in prison and tortured, or sometimes killed. Saul hoped that this would stop people becoming 'Followers of the Way', as they were called at the time. Many of them left Jerusalem to avoid getting caught.

The High Priest was delighted when Saul asked for permission to follow some of the believers to Damascus, and bring them back to Jerusalem as prisoners.

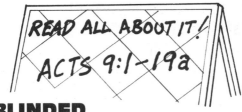

READ ALL ABOUT IT!
ACTS 9:1–19a

BLINDED

When he got near to Damascus, a bright light suddenly flashed all around him and he fell to the ground, blinded. Then he heard a voice saying to him,

'Saul, why are you going on persecuting me?'

'Who are you, Lord?'
was Saul's reply. He was told that it was Jesus speaking to him. Saul was to get up, and go on to Damascus where he would be told what to do next.

Saul's companions had to lead him into Damascus. For three days he stayed in the house of a man called Judas in Straight Street. He refused all the food and drink which he was offered.

A Jewish boy reading from a Hebrew text

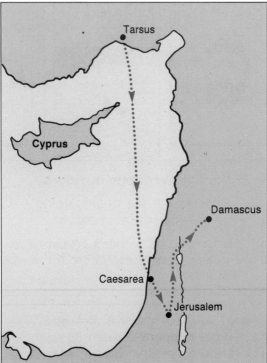

B Straight Street, Damascus

Saul travelled to Damascus to persecute the Christians.

SAUL BECOMES A CHRISTIAN

On the other side of Damascus, Ananias was praying to God. He was told to find Saul who would be told that a man called Ananias was coming to restore his sight. Ananias had heard that Saul was coming to Damascus, and so he wasn't too keen on visiting Saul, but God told him that he had chosen Saul to tell the Gentiles about Jesus.

Ananias did as he was instructed, and went to Saul. When he arrived, he called Saul his brother, and laid his hands on Saul's eyes. Immediately, Saul could see again. He also knew that he would be spending the rest of his life following Jesus. Ananias **baptized** Saul, who then spent several days with the other believers in Damascus. He even started to preach about Jesus in the **synagogues** there.

He had gone to Damascus to persecute Christians. When he left there, he was a Christian himself.

NOTES/DATABASE

Use the glossary to look up the meanings of the following words. Then use the definitions to make your own notes or suitable entries on your database.

Gentiles	Persecution
Rabbi	Baptized
Pharisee	Synagogue

ACTIVITIES

1 Quick quiz

a What was Paul's Jewish name?

b Using the map, and atlas, find out what Turkey used to be called.

c What had Saul planned for his career?

d Why was Saul shocked when he heard Christians praying to Jesus?

e Why did Saul wish to persecute the Christians?

f What happened to those Christians who were caught?

g Name the town to which Saul was told to go.

h What was the name of the street where he stayed?

i What was Ananias doing when he was told to find Saul?

j Why do you think Ananias was not too keen on seeing Saul?

k What did Ananias call Saul?

l What did Ananias do to Saul immediately after he could see again?

m How did Saul show that he really had become a Christian himself?

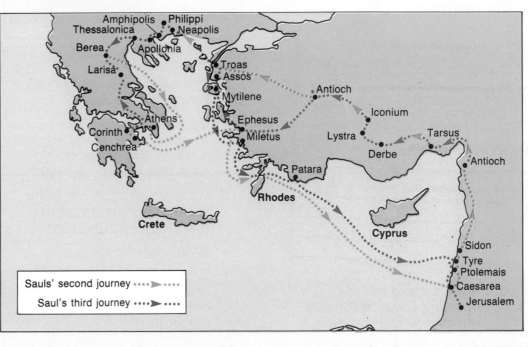

Sauls' second journey ····▸····
Saul's third journey ····▸····

FURTHER ACTIVITIES

OVER THE WALL

1 Read Acts 9:19–25 carefully.

a How do you think the believers in Damascus felt when they knew that Saul was coming to try to capture them?

b Why do you think the Jews wanted to kill Saul? (Verse 22)

c Imagine you are one of Saul's friends. You have heard that the Jews are planning to kill him. Write the story of how you made your plans to get Saul out of Damascus.

ARE YOU A MEMBER OF A CLUB?

2 Fill in a membership certificate for yourself.

> **MEMBERSHIP CERTIFICATE**
>
> ....CLUB
>
> NAME ....
>
> AGE ....
>
> DATE OF JOINING ....
>
> SPECIAL INTERESTS ....
>
> ....
>
> AWARDS GAINED (E.g. Scout or Guide badges, Duke of Edinburgh awards etc.)
>
> ....
>
> ....

a If someone said lots of unpleasant things about your club, how would you feel?

b If that person wanted to join, how would you react?

c If a friend, who was a member, came to you and said 'Let him join, he has really changed', would this help?

d Why wouldn't the rest of the disciples in Jerusalem believe that Saul was a Christian?

e Who spoke up for Saul?

f What did Saul do as soon as he was accepted as a member of the Church by the rest of the disciples?

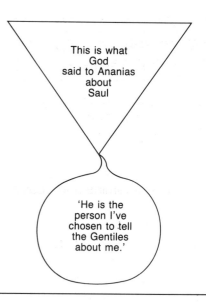

This is what God said to Ananias about Saul

'He is the person I've chosen to tell the Gentiles about me.'

When Greeks started hearing about Jesus, the Church in Jerusalem sent Barnabas to investigate.

3 a What kind of person was Barnabas?

b Find out what people said about Barnabas. Look in Acts 11:22–24.

Barnabas knew that God had chosen Saul for the work of telling the Gentiles about Jesus, so he sent for Saul. They worked together in Antioch for a year.

How many of us have to die before the world will help us?

HOW DO YOU USUALLY FIND OUT ABOUT FAMINES?

4 a Make a list of the ways in which you find out about famines.

b Make a list of the ways in which people now help in times of famine and disaster.

5 Read Acts 11:27–30.

a How did the early Church find out there was going to be a famine?

b Did this prophecy come true? If so, when?

c What did they decide to do about it?

d What similarities are there in the ways in which countries like England help in times of famine and the ways in which the Church in Antioch helped?

e Explain how an understanding of the ways the early Church responded to the famine could help a Church now to decide how they could help.

C 'I was hungry and you fed me' JESUS

OFF ON THEIR TRAVELS

6 Read Acts 13:1–3.

a What was the Church in Antioch doing when they were told to send Saul and Barnabas off on their journey?

b Who told them to select those two people?

c What did the Church do to commission Saul and Barnabas for this particular work?

NEWS FROM LYSTRA

HAVE THE GODS RETURNED?

> We are not gods or even very good people!

TEMPLE OF ZEUS

STONED AND LEFT FOR DEAD

Tuesday

A wandering Jewish preacher from Tarsus was today stoned and left for dead outside the city of Lystra. This fake has been pretending to be a religious teacher. His pretence came to an end when Jewish leaders arrived in Lystra and informed the authorities that he was a con-man. Earlier he had claimed to heal a man with deformed feet. How this trick was performed has not yet been discovered. Paul was stoned. He was believed to be dead, but there have been reports that he returned briefly to the city before leaving for Derbe.

Monday

A man with deformed feet was healed here in Lystra earlier this week. This amazing event took place in front of hundreds of our citizens. Only the gods could do this! The gods Zeus and Hermes seem to have returned in human form. With the true humility we should expect from gods, they refused to allow the chief priest of the Temple of Zeus to put wreaths on them and sacrifice to them. They insisted that they were two servants of a Jewish god named Jesus. They claim this Jesus was the one who really healed the man with the deformed feet!

Read Acts 14:8–20 carefully, as well as the newspaper reports on this page.

7 Imagine that you are a Christian from the Church in Lystra.

Write in to the newspaper giving your version of the events in Lystra.

When Paul and Barnabas returned to Jerusalem, they told the **Apostles** about the **Gentile** believers in Jesus. Some people started to say that all Gentile believers had to keep the **Jewish Law**. Paul and Barnabas were involved in some fierce arguments about this. Eventually the Apostles decided to send a letter to the Gentile believers which said that they did not have to keep the food laws.

After this, Paul decided to go on another journey. This time his friend Silas went with him, while Barnabas sailed off to Cyprus with John Mark.

INTO EUROPE

While they were in Troas (in Asia Minor, or Turkey), Paul had a vision of a Greek person from Macedonia saying, 'Come over to Macedonia to help us'. This seems to be the point when Luke, who wrote the account of Paul's journeys, joined them.

A Europe from Asia

LYDIA BECOMES A CHRISTIAN

The first person to believe in Jesus in Greece was someone called Lydia. She was a **'God-fearer'**, someone who worshipped the Jewish God. In the Jewish religion, women are not allowed to hold **synagogue** services unless there are ten men present. A group of women in Philippi wanted to pray together, so they met by the river. Paul went to find them, and he told them about Jesus. Lydia, who was a rich lady, a trader in purple cloth, not only believed in Jesus, but also invited Paul to stay at her house. Read the story for yourself in Acts 16:11 – 15.

MORE JOURNEYS

Paul had many adventures as he told people about Jesus. He went on three **missionary** journeys altogether, as well as a final trip to Rome. During this time, he was imprisoned several times, flogged, and sometimes chased out of town. He even managed to cause a riot!

LETTER WRITING

As he went on these journeys, he started new churches, all over Greece as well as Turkey. Sometimes the Christians in these new churches found it difficult to know how to behave as **Christians**, and Paul wrote to them to give advice as well as to keep in touch. There are thirteen letters in the New Testament which he signed. The other Apostles did this too. There are also two letters written by Peter, and three by John. James, who might have been a brother of Jesus, also wrote a letter. Even when Paul was in prison he went on writing letters to the Christians around the world. He never sounded sorry for himself even if he was stuck in a cell at the time.

THE FAMINE

Paul never forgot that there was going to be a famine. When the famine came, he had collected a large amount of money for the poor people who lived in the area near Jerusalem. He decided to take it there himself. He was warned by many people that he would probably be imprisoned if he returned to Jerusalem. Agabus, the same prophet who had foretold the famine, came to see Paul in Caesarea. He took Paul's own belt and tied it around his feet and hands and said: 'The owner of this belt will be tied up like this by the Jews in Jerusalem, they will hand him over to the Gentiles' (Acts 21:11).

JERUSALEM AND IMPRISONMENT

In spite of these warnings, Paul went on to Jerusalem with the money to help the victims of the famine.

Paul was advised by James and the leaders of the church in Jerusalem to go to the Temple for seven days to make an offering. Paul took their advice, but on the seventh day, some Jews from Asia arrived and stirred everyone up against Paul. He was arrested and handed over to the Romans.

For two years, Paul was in prison in Caesarea. Eventually there was a new

B Greek remains from the time of St Paul

trial with some Jews making serious accusations against him. It was Paul's right, as a Roman citizen, to be tried by the Emperor. Paul therefore said, 'I appeal to Caesar'. The Roman governor had to send him to Rome.

On the way to Rome, Paul was shipwrecked and had many more adventures. Finally he arrived in Rome.

NOTES/DATABASE

Use the glossary to look up the meanings of the following words. Then use the definitions to make your own notes or suitable entries on your database.

Apostles	Synagogue
Gentile	Missionary
Jewish Law	Christian
God-fearer	

1 Quick quiz

a What did Paul and Barnabas often find they were involved in arguments about?

b How did the Apostles overcome this problem?

c How was Paul told that the next place he had to go to was Macedonia?

d Who joined Paul on his journey to Macedonia?

e Who was the first person to believe in Jesus in Greece?

f Why did a group of women pray together near a river rather than in a synagogue?

g How many missionary journeys did Paul go on?

h Why did Paul write letters to the people in Greece after he had set up churches there?

i Why was it necessary for Paul to collect a large sum of money?

j Why was Paul warned against returning to Jerusalem?

k What did Agabus say would happen to Paul?

l How many days did Paul visit the Temple before he was arrested?

m How long was Paul in prison in Caesarea?

n Why did the Roman governor have to send Paul to Rome for his trial?

o What happened on the way to Rome?

ACTIVITIES

EARTHQUAKE!

Can you believe it?
An earthquake hit the town of Philippi during the night. It measured 9 on the Richter scale. Many buildings were demolished, including part of the prison. No prisoners chose to escape, despite their cell being blown open.

Group work

2 Read Acts 16:16–28.

A Design a series of pictures for a filmstrip showing:

a Why Paul and Silas got arrested this time (verse 16–24).

b What happened when the earthquake came (verse 25f).

c Why the jailor became a Christian (verse 27f).

d Why Paul insisted that the magistrates came to escort himself and Silas out of prison (verse 37).

B Write down, then record (using several different voices and interesting dialogue) a script for your filmstrip.

If you can use an overhead projector, you might be able to arrange to draw your pictures on OHP transparencies. Then you would be able to present your pictures and the tape recording together, to help other people understand this story.

FURTHER ACTIVITIES

'TO AN UNKNOWN GOD'

1 Read Acts 17:16–34.

a What was Paul distressed about while he was waiting in Athens?

b Where did he have discussions every day?

c Why do you think that the market place was a popular place to exchange ideas?

d What did Paul say about the 'unknown God'?

e Why do you think that some people sneered at the idea of the Resurrection?

2 a How do you react when you hear someone preaching in the street?

b Do you think that people reacted in a similar way to Paul?

c How did Paul get their attention?

3 Imagine that Paul came to your school. Write a speech which he might have made in assembly telling you about Jesus.

C The Parthenon – a temple to the Greek gods

Did you know?

A **stoic** was someone who struggled on, whatever problems he might meet.

Did you know?

An **epicurean** was someone who was only interested in pleasure!

I wonder which I am?

PUBLIC MEETING

Silversmith's Takings Down!
We have always made high quality models of the goddess Diana here in Ephesus. The perfection of our craftsmanship has made them into a steady source of income. Paul's preaching is ruining our trade. A public meeting will be held at noon today to decide what action to take. *Demetrius.*

4 Read Acts 19:23–41 carefully.

a Why did Demetrius hold a public meeting?

b What reason did he give for the drop in trade?

c Do you think he was more interested in the drop in trade or the honour of the goddess Diana?

d What similarities can you see between the public meeting Demetrius held and ones which are held now?

D Stall selling religious artefacts

5 a Why do you think Paul was prevented from going to the theatre?

b Why do you think the crowd would not let Alexander speak?

c How did the city clerk quieten the crowd down?

d Do you think that the city clerk was right when he suggested that the affair should be dealt with in a court of law?

e Explain why Paul's preaching about Jesus could have affected the silversmith's trade.

APPEAL TO CAESAR

Paul was a Roman citizen. He had the right to be tried by Caesar himself. So when he appealed to Caesar, he had to go to Rome. But read Acts 26–32 to find out what King Agrippa thought about the affair.

NEWS OF THE EMPIRE

PAUL APPEALS TO CAESAR

Read Acts 27 very carefully.

6 Use Acts 27 to write the Captain's log of the voyage until they are shipwrecked off Malta.

CAPTAIN'S LOG

Voyage to Rome

Day One

Centurion Julius and some prisoners joined the ship. One of the prisoners, a Roman citizen called Paul of Tarsus is on his way to Rome for trial before Caesar himself. – don't like the responsibility.

PAUL SHIPWRECKED!

E First century ship

7 a Design some luggage labels for Paul's journey to Rome, showing the places he stopped at. Use travel brochures and an atlas to find out enough about the places, including Malta and Syracuse to draw good labels. Puteoli is now called Pozzuoli and is near Naples.

Map work

b Use an atlas and the map on page 73 to draw your own map of the route which Paul took to Rome. All the information you need is in Acts 27–28.

WELCOME TO ROME, THE ETERNAL CITY.

F The Bell at Lloyds of London, rung only when a ship is lost

A The Forum

GOOD NEWS IN ROME

Luke's story ends when the Good News about Jesus has reached Rome. When people in Rome knew about Jesus, then, from Luke's point of view, the story was complete.

PAUL'S LETTERS

Paul went on writing letters to Christians in the places where he had told them about Jesus. These groups of Christians became known as '**Churches**'. When Paul writes about a Church, he never means the building. He always means the people. Sometimes he had to deal with difficulties and divisions in the Church. This was what happened at

B Roman ruins in Herculaneum

Corinth. People formed little groups and started saying that one group was better than another. Paul wrote to them to try and help them to understand that Jesus wanted them all to be united, and not quarrelling with one another. (You can look this up in I Corinthians 1:10–13.)

Paul was very keen that everyone in the Church should realize that they all had their part to play. He wrote to them about 'gifts' or **talents**, which everyone has.

Paul's letters show his concern for the people who became Christians. Many of the new Christians had been slaves. There were lots of women who became Christians. It was the only religion which treated everyone as equals, and this was part of the reason that ordinary working people became Christians. You didn't have to be any special kind of person to be a Christian. You simply needed to believe in Jesus and to know that God loved you. With the **Gospels**, these letters are still the basis of all Christian teaching.

We don't know exactly what happened to Paul. He stayed in Rome for two years at least (Acts 28:30). Some people think that he might have gone to Spain to tell people about Jesus. There is a very strong tradition that he was in Rome during the time when the Emperor Nero **persecuted** Christians. This happened after the great fire of Rome in 64 CE. Tacitus, a Roman writer, tells us that Nero was believed to have started the fire himself, and stirred up the people of Rome against Christians to avoid taking the blame. It is likely that Paul was beheaded during this troubled period.

PETER

Peter went to Rome too. It is believed that he was the first Bishop of Rome. There are two letters signed by him in the New Testament. I Peter was obviously written at a time when Christians were being persecuted.

Being a Christian in Rome in those days was a risky business. The Emperor of Rome believed he was a god, and everyone had to offer incense in front of a statue of Caesar and worship him. Christians were not prepared to do this. If they were caught and imprisoned, they were likely to be executed. Many of them died. Some were thrown to the lions in Rome, in the Circus Maximus or the Colosseum. Some were made to fight gladiators. Many Christians hid in the catacombs, the underground burial places on the road called the Appian Way.

Peter, tradition tells us, was eventually caught. There is an interesting story which people told about his death. Peter was escaping from Rome along the Appian Way, when he met a man coming towards him. As he looked more closely, the man turned out to be Jesus. 'Where are you going Lord?' Peter asked. 'I'm going to Rome to be crucified instead of you', Jesus answered. So Peter returned to Rome and was imprisoned and **crucified**. Peter chose to be crucified upside down because he did not feel good enough to die in the same way as Jesus.

C The tomb of Cecilia Metalla

NOTES/DATABASE

Use the glossary to look up the meanings of the following words. Then use the definitions to make your own notes or suitable entries on your database.

Church   Persecuted

Talents   Crucified

Gospel

ACTIVITIES

1 **Quick quiz**

a When did Luke's story finish?

b Who did Paul write his letters to?

c What is the real meaning of the word 'Church'?

d Why did Paul have to write and explain that he wanted Christians to be united?

e How did Paul help everyone in the Church realize they all had a part to play?

f Give one way in which Christianity is different from other religions.

g How long does Luke tell us that Paul was in Rome?

h Who did Tacitus believe had started the fire of Rome?

i What was the reason Tacitus would have given for this belief?

j How do we think Paul died?

k Who do we believe was the first Bishop of Rome?

l Why was it a risky business being a Christian in Rome in those days?

D The Colosseum

m What sometimes happened to Christians who were caught?

n Where did the Christians sometimes hide?

o Why, according to the story, was Peter travelling along the Appian Way when he met Jesus?

p Why did Peter turn round and return to Rome?

q How did Peter die?

Although some Christians were wealthy, many of them were slaves. They had to meet before dawn to pray, and then go back to the wealthy households in which they were slaves to do a day's work.

When Nero started to persecute the Christians, they often met in the catacombs to pray. This made some people more scared of Christians, because they were already nervous about the catacombs as these were underground burial chambers.

It was therefore dangerous to be a Christian, so they began to have secret signs to find out if someone was a Christian.

Here are some of their secret signs:

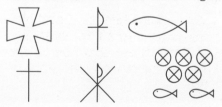

Some of these are scratched on the walls of first century prisons and other buildings. This ancient graffiti shows Christians were there.

2 Use the information on this page to write a story in which you imagine you are a Christian living in Rome in 64 CE.

FURTHER ACTIVITIES

BELONGING
(I Corinthians 12)

For discussion

1 a Have you ever felt that you don't belong?

  b Do you ever sit in a lesson and think what you have to say is not important?

  c Do you ever feel that certain people are always the ones who answer questions, or talk and have ideas on all sorts of subjects?

E Children in a gymnasium

F Pit stop in motor racing

Paul says that everyone should take part in a Church. He makes it clear that everyone has a useful part to play. Read I Corinthians 12.

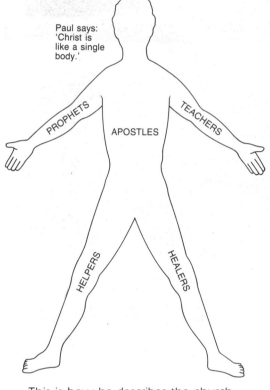

Paul says: 'Christ is like a single body.'

PROPHETS

APOSTLES

TEACHERS

HELPERS

HEALERS

This is how he describes the church
The whole body is the church (remember that means people, not a building).

Ephesians 4:11–16. Paul says the same thing in different words.

2 **Think of the various jobs (including being a pupil) which there are in your school.**

Design a diagram like Paul's description of the Church which shows how everyone in your school is necessary for its smooth running.

PAUL'S TEACHING ABOUT LOVE

Read carefully what Paul says about love in I Corinthians 13.

Love is patient, Love is kind.
It does not envy, it does not boast.
It is not rude, it is not self-seeking.
It is not easily angered.
It keeps no record of wrongs.
Love does not delight in evil,
but rejoices in the truth.
It always protects, always trusts,
always hopes, always perseveres.
Love never fails.

Paul of Tarsus.

Greek words for love:
phileo . . . friendship on an equal basis,
eros . . . sexual love,
agape . . . real love expressed in caring for others in every way.

The kind of love Paul is talking about in I Corinthians 12 is *agape*, the caring kind of love.

3 a Using verses 4–7, make a list of the things which Paul says about love.

b Use these to design your own, new style 'Love is . . .' cards.

4 Look carefully at these pictures.

Now discuss and write down ways in which they show *agape* love being put into practice.

G Missionary working in Ethiopia

For discussion

5 What divisions are there in the world today which prevent people from being equal?

'In Christ there are no divisions between Jews and Gentiles, between slaves and free people, between men and women. Everyone is exactly the same'.

Galatians 3:28

This equality between people is one of the basic beliefs of Christianity. In the Roman world, there were many divisions such as those listed by Paul. This was one of the reasons so many people wanted to become Christians.

H He's my brother

6 How would you rewrite the above quotation (Galatians 3:28) to make sense in today's world?

Write down your reasons for choosing these particular categories.

I Martin Luther King

'I have a dream that my four children will one day live in a nation where they will not be judged by the colour of their skin, but by the content of their character'

Martin Luther King

Martin Luther King was a black Christian civil rights leader who spoke out for equality for everyone –

for rich and poor

for black and white.

He was assassinated in 1968 in Memphis, Tennesee.

LOVE IS
Something
which never fails

THE BEGINNING

Whatever people believe about Jesus of Nazareth, there can be no doubt that he changed the world. He has been more influential than any man who ever lived, before, or since.

There is no doubt that he was an historical person. There is better evidence that he really lived than there is for Julius Caesar, and many other famous people in history.

The world is a very different place because of the life of Jesus. He taught love and equality and caring for others as no-one else has ever done. The Apostles who were sent out to tell the world about him did a good job. Within 300 years, Christianity became the official religion of the Roman Empire.

Ambassador   Representative of king or country in a foreign land

Anointed   Kings are anointed at their coronation

Apostle   Someone sent out with a special message

Ascension   The time when Jesus returned to Heaven

Baptized   Using water as a sign that someone has changed their way of life

Bishop   A church leader in Orthodox, Catholic and Anglican traditions with oversight of an area

Christ   Greek word meaning 'anointed'. See also Messiah

Christian   Word first used at Antioch to describe the followers of Jesus. Before this they were called 'Followers of the Way'

Church   A group of people who meet together to worship Jesus

Commandments   The rules which God gave the people of Israel to help them to serve Him

Confirmation   The second part of baptism, when a bishop lays hands on someone

Crucifixion, crucified   Method of execution used by the Romans of nailing someone to a cross

Deacon   Greek word meaning 'servant'. Used to describe people chosen to help the disciples. Later an order of Ministry

Disciple   Someone who is learning

Essenes   The religious community who lived near the Dead Sea and wrote the Dead Sea Scrolls

Eucharist   Word for service which remembers Jesus' Last Supper with his disciples which really means 'Thanksgiving'

Feast of Dedication   Jewish festival in which people carried palm branches to the Temple.

Feast of Pentecost   a) Jewish festival remembering gift of Ten commandments b) Christian festival remembering gift of Holy Spirit

Gentile   Someone who is not a Jew

Gethsemane   An olive grove at the bottom of the Mount of Olives, where Jesus went to pray on the night he was betrayed by Judas

God-fearer   Someone who was not Jewish who believed in the God of Israel

Golgotha   Word meaning 'Place of the Skull'. Name for the place of execution in Jerusalem

Gospel   Word meaning 'Good News'. Usually means the Good News about Jesus. Also the books of the New Testament, Matthew, Mark, Luke and John, which tell us about the life of Jesus

Hebrew   The language in which the Old Testament was written, and still spoken by Jews today

High Priest   Leader of the Sanhedrin, or Jewish religious Council, usually a Sadducee

Holy Communion   Word used by Anglicans and others for service which remembers the Last Supper which Jesus had with his disciples

Holy Spirit   The presence of God

Holy Week   The last week that Jesus spent in Jerusalem before he was crucified

Jew   A descendant of Abraham

Jewish Law (Torah), religious law   Laws which the Jews had which helped them to serve God better

Judaism   The belief of the Jews

Kiddush   A little meal eaten after a synagogue service or festival. Word really means 'Blessing'

Kingdom of God   The rule of God

Kosher   Food prepared according to Jewish religious law

Lord's Prayer   The family prayer of the Church which Jesus taught to his disciples

Lord's Supper   Word used by Free Churches to describe the service which remembers Jesus' Last Supper with his disciples

Mass   Word used by Roman Catholics to describe the service which remembers Jesus' Last Supper with his disciples

Messiah   The person expected by the Jews to help them and lead them. Word is Hebrew for 'anointed'

Ministry   The time when Jesus was showing the world who he was, and telling them about God

Miracle   An amazing event initiated by God

Missionary   Someone who is sent out by a Church with the job of telling others about Jesus

Mount Zion   One of the seven hills of Jerusalem on which King David was buried, and where Jesus ate the Passover meal

Myrrh   A plant used as a pain killing drug

Ordination   Ceremony at which someone receives the Church's authority to do the work Jesus gave to his disciples

Parable   A way of explaining a difficult idea in a story about very ordinary things

Passion Narrative   The part of the Gospels which tell about Jesus' last week in Jerusalem, his death and Resurrection

Passover   Jewish festival to remember the escape of the Israelites from Egypt

Persecution, Persecuted   When someone is mistreated, imprisoned, tortured or discriminated against because of their beliefs

Pharisee   A religious leader who kept the Jewish law in all its detail, and who believed in the Resurrection

Pilgrim   Someone who goes on a journey for religious reasons

Pope   The leader of the Roman Catholic Church

Priest   In Orthodox, Catholic and Anglican traditions, a priest is someone set apart by the Church to do the work which Jesus gave to his disciples

Promised Land   The land which God promised to Abraham (Genesis 12:4)

Prophecy   What a prophet says

Prophet   Someone who explains the word of God for his times

Rabbi   A Jewish religious leader, who was not a priest

Resurrection   Returning to life, after someone has died. Usually applied to Jesus

Sabbath   The seventh day, on which working was forbidden

Sacrifice   Offering animals or produce in the Temple, in order to say either 'Thank you' or 'Sorry' to God

Sadducee   A member of the ruling class, usually a priest, usually rich. Did not believe in the Resurrection

Samaritan   Someone who lived in Samaria. They were similar to Jews except that they disagreed about where to worship God

Saviour   If someone was drowning and you jumped in to help them, you would be their saviour

Scribe   Someone who wrote things down, and who advised people about the religious law

Scriptures   The Old Testament

Seder   Passover meal (word really means 'order')

Shalom   Hebrew word of 'Peace', used by Jewish people instead of 'Hello'

Shema   The words of Deuteronomy 6:4, 5 which Jews say every day

Sukkot   Festival at which the Jews thanked God for leading them out of Egypt

Synagogue   The building in which Jews meet to worship God

Talents   Gifts or abilities which someone has been given

Tax collector   Someone who worked for the Romans by collecting the taxes

Temple   Central place of Jewish worship where animals were sacrificed. The Jerusalem Temple was destroyed in 70 CE and never rebuilt

Transfiguration   The time when Jesus took some disciples to the top of a mountain and appeared to them as a shining figure

Unleavened bread   Bread which has not risen because it contains no yeast